DREAMS

Every night we dream, ar ~~~~ **have more than 150,000 dreams. All dreams—even nightmares—contain positive messages, but how do you unlock these keys to self-discovery?**

What does it mean if you dream about a goddess? Or that you possess supernatural powers? What do these visions reveal about the real events in your life? The trick is learning to decipher the symbolism so you can understand what your dreams are telling you. Based on the latest scientific research, DREAMS & NIGHTMARES is an engaging revelation of the sleeping mind. The Dreams half explores the nature of dreams and the reasons why you have them. With the help of interpretations from Freud, Jung, and present-day dream theorists, it investigates the generally accepted meanings of 50 dream symbols, conveniently grouped by theme. Unlock the power of dreams and discover how to:

- Clarify what dreams are and why you have them.

- Use your dreams to gain insight into your life.

- Explore common dream symbols such as angels, various animals, and heroes.

- Examine universal dream experiences such as traveling, flying, and being someone else.

- Keep a dream journal and discover patterns in your dreams.

This fascinating book will take you on a journey of discovery that is sure to absorb, entertain, and enlighten you.

ABOUT THE AUTHOR

Jennifer Parker, Ph.D., is a senior lecturer in research methods, consciousness studies, and addiction studies at the University of the West of England. Parker has researched dreams for 15 years and is a longstanding member of the International Association for the Study of Dreams and

DREAMS
& NIGHTMARES

Discover What Your
Dreams Are Telling You

JENNIFER PARKER, Ph.D.

ILLUSTRATED BY CATHERINE McINTYRE

The Reader's Digest Association, Inc.

Pleasantville, New York | Montreal | Sydney | Singapore | Mumbai

A READER'S DIGEST BOOK

This edition published by The Reader's Digest Association, Inc., by arrangement with Ivy Press.

Library of Congress Cataloging-in-Publication Data

Parker, Jennifer
  Dreams & nightmares : discover what your dreams are telling you, discover what your nightmares are telling you / Jennifer Parker.
    p. cm.
  ISBN 978-1-60652-166-3
1. Dreams. 2. Nightmares. I. Title.
II. Title: Dreams and nightmares.
  BF1078.P315 2010
  154.6'3--dc22

                    2010003348

We are committed to both the quality of our products and the service we provide to our customers. We value your comments, so please feel free to contact us.

   The Reader's Digest Association, Inc.
   Adult Trade Publishing
   Reader's Digest Road
   Pleasantville, NY 10570–7000

For more Reader's Digest products and information, visit our website:

   www.rd.com (in the United States)
   www.readersdigest.ca (in Canada)
   www.readersdigest.co.uk (in the UK)
   www.rdasia.com (in Asia)

Printed in China

Color Origination by Ivy Press Reprographics

1 3 5 7 9 10 8 6 4 2

This book was conceived, designed, and produced by
Ivy Press
210 High Street, Lewes
East Sussex BN7 2NS, U.K.

FOR IVY PRESS
PUBLISHER Jason Hook
ART DIRECTOR Michael Whitehead
EDITORIAL DIRECTOR Caroline Earle
DESIGNER JC Lanaway
ILLUSTRATOR Catherine McIntyre

FOR READER'S DIGEST
U.S. PROJECT EDITOR Siobhan Sullivan
CANADIAN PROJECT MANAGER Pamela Johnson
CANADIAN PROJECT EDITOR Jesse Corbeil
PROJECT DESIGNER Jennifer Tokarski
SENIOR ART DIRECTOR George McKeon
EXECUTIVE EDITOR, TRADE PUBLISHING Dolores York
ASSOCIATE PUBLISHER, TRADE PUBLISHING Rosanne McManus
PRESIDENT AND PUBLISHER, TRADE PUBLISHING Harold Clarke

Contents

Dreams

Who are you in your dreams? Where do you go? Can you make sense of your nighttime visions? Dreaming is a mysterious, vital part of the human experience, which is documented in some of the oldest books and records. Our fascination with dreams is nothing new. Millennia ago our ancestors understood that dreams were important. Ancient philosophers, such as Hippocrates and Aristotle, debated whether they were caused by the positions of the stars, or by bodily processes. In China, up to the sixteenth century, many believed they shouldn't make important decisions until they had a dream that was suitably auspicious.

Our dreams are shape-shifting but revealing mirrors. They reflect our changing mental states and take us to worlds where the impossible is possible, where our wildest fears and desires come out to play, and the rules of our earthbound lives no longer apply.

What Is a Dream?

The dreams we remember can range in complexity from fleeting images to long, convoluted, and complex stories. A memorable dream may constitute a single, static image that is all the dreamer's conscious mind is able to retrieve from a larger dreaming experience. Or, often we grasp the end of a complex dream as we awake, knowing there was more to the dream than we can recall. A dream as we remember it is rarely the whole story.

In a typical dream, the dreamer is not aware that he or she is dreaming. Dreamers are completely absorbed in the dream's events, and they have no sense of unreality. For this reason, dreams can be called hallucinatory experiences. A dreamer is unable to direct events or make things happen. With rare exceptions, the dream unfolds beyond the control of the dreamer, who has no choice but to go along with what happens. Because the decision- and action-taking parts of the brain are switched off, there is no option to leave the scene by waking up.

The sleep cycle

There are five stages of sleep that researchers have identified by measuring levels of electrical activity. They use three electro-physiological measurements to assess what the body does while we sleep. An electroencephalogram (EEG) measures brain activity, an electrooccculargram (EOG) measures eye movement, while an electromyogram (EMG) measures muscle tone around the chin. During stage 1 of sleep, we settle down and relax, and this is always a light sleep. During the next phase, stage 2, we are fully asleep and shut out the outside world completely.

Sleep patterns across a "normal" night's sleep

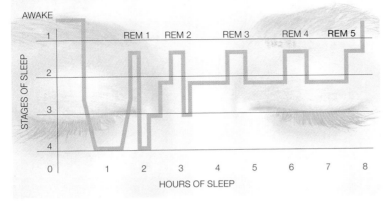

Sleep cycles change through the night. In the first half, NREM sleep dominates, and we dream for about five minutes at the end of the cycle. In the second half, we have more REM sleep, during which we are more likely to dream.

During stages 3 and 4, we are in deep sleep and metabolic levels slow down. Stage 5 is known as delta or rapid eye movement (REM) sleep, and dreaming is most associated with this final stage. The four previous sleep stages are nonrapid eye movement (NREM) sleep. This is characterized by slow brain activity, rolling eye movements, and the presence of muscle tone. REM sleep is identifiable by fast brain waves, the kind of eye movements you would use to follow a moving object, and the absence of muscle tone. Our brains work as they do when we are awake, but because our muscles do not function, we cannot move and hurt ourselves.

We undergo these five stages, or sleep cycles, several times during the night. Each cycle lasts about 90 minutes. We are more likely to remember a dream first thing in the morning after the longest period of REM sleep.

Case Study

In Ruth's waking life, she carried around the snapshot of a dream that never left her. She was aware that the original dream had been much longer, but all Ruth could remember was a single image of a stonefish. Ruth was so haunted by this dream that she discussed it with the dream analyst, Dr. Michael Conforti, and together they were able to derive meaning from her memory. A stonefish—an especially poisonous fish— lives in a harsh and inhospitable environment, where any other fish would perish. Ruth was a survivor of the Holocaust. As she talked through her thoughts with Conforti, she realized that the stonefish, with its negative connotations, encapsulated the feelings of guilt and isolation that she still suffered as a result of her traumatic experiences.

What Does a Typical Dream Contain?

Dream researchers have established that about 95 percent of dreams contain visual imagery. In the remaining 5 percent of dreams, the dreamer may sense only a taste, a touch, or a voice. Most dreams also contain at least one setting and one change in location. The location changes are sometimes achieved by the dreamer taking a form of transport and at other times by the dreamer simply walking from one place to another. Typically dreams contain at least two characters apart from the dreamer, and there is a 50 percent chance that one of these characters will be known to the dreamer. Close family members or partners, however, only feature in about 15 percent of dream reports, whereas there is a 30 percent chance that a dream will contain strangers, or characters of uncertain identity. This may be the brain's way of allowing us to explore what we don't know rather than what we do, or in the case of nightmares, it may suggest that it is easier to accept violence or threat from an unknown aggressor rather than someone who is known to us.

Most people's dreams contain at least one setting, as well as visual imagery. The vast majority of recorded dreams include at least two other characters in addition to the dreamer.

The dreamer's experience

When quizzed about the content of their dreams, people often report achieving a goal, such as opening a locked door. Experiencing a misfortune, such as having an illness or a broken-down car, is also common. Less frequently, dreamers report good fortune, such as finding money. Failure, such as buying a lottery ticket but not winning, is also less common. Interestingly considering the personal nature of dreams, emotion is referred to in only one in three dream reports, unless the dreamer is specifically asked what he or she was feeling during the dream.

Typically, a recalled dream will involve the dreamer interacting with other dream characters. These interactions can be broadly categorized into three types: aggressive interactions are the most common; sexual interactions take place the least frequently; and the incidence of friendly dream interactions comes somewhere between the two. The position of the dreamer in the interaction is also revealing. For example, the dreamer may be the aggressor, or the victim of aggression; in friendly interactions, the dreamer may

Twelve universal dream themes

Garfield's list allows us to begin to think about the ways we share dream experiences.

- Being embraced or feeling love
- Being healed or reborn
- Experiencing pleasure
- Improvement
- Good performance

- Flying, swimming, or dancing
- Being well-dressed in public
- Smooth operation (of machinery/technology)

- Natural beauty and miracles
- Discovering new spaces
- Receiving guidance
- Pleasant journeys

be the initiator or may be on the receiving end of kind behavior. It is possible to analyze each aspect of a dream separately. Therefore, anyone who is trying to work out what a dream really means has a great deal of information to consider in his or her interpretation. As the case study on page 7 shows, even a single image can carry many different meanings.

Universal dream themes

Over the years, dream researchers have identified a number of universal dream themes. Regardless of location, cultural background, or social status, people describe certain strikingly similar dreams over and over.

One of the best accounts of universal dreams was published in 2001 by Patricia Garfield, a prolific dream researcher who was the cofounder of the International Association for the Study of Dreams in the United States. She drew up a list of 12 positive universal dream themes—see box above.

An earlier dream study that was carried out in Japan and the United States in 1958 named other universal dream themes that Patricia Garfield did not include in her classification. These included eating delicious food, swimming in bodies of calm water, falling without fear, flying, and sex. Additional themes emerged when the same survey was repeated in 1996, including interacting with famous characters. The majority of universal dream themes, however, seem to remain constant. We can only guess whether they will stay that way in future.

Can dream sharing help to overcome barriers?

In 2006 a dream workshop was held in a detention center for young male offenders from both Catholic and Protestant backgrounds in Northern Ireland. The dream worker gradually persuaded the teenagers to share their dream experiences. As they opened up, the boys realized that, despite their different faiths, they shared the same aspirations—and the same fears. Aggression in the detention center was reduced significantly as a result of the workshop.

The Sexes & Dreams

Men and women have different types of dreams, and they talk about their dreams differently. Women tend to be more interested in their dream lives, and they tend to share their dreams more often. One of the most famous studies in dream research history was conducted by Calvin Hall and Robert Van de Castle in 1966. In this study 100 men and 100 women from California were each asked to report five dreams. The results of this pivotal study give us a clear idea of what typical male and female dreams are.

Can we ever share the same dreams at the same time?

Research by Professor Mark Blagrove at the University of Swansea, Wales, suggests that couples do not share dreams. This finding contradicts anecdotal evidence and a popularly held belief that if two people are close enough, they will meet in their dreams as a continuation of their waking relationship.

Men's dreams

In the typical dreams of men, the most frequent characters are other men that the dreamer knows. The most common type of social interaction involves aggression, and the dreamer is more commonly the victim. In approximately half of aggression dreams, a physical attack is involved. Aggressive interactions usually involve men the dreamer doesn't know, whereas friendly interactions most often occur with women. In these scenarios, the dreamer is usually protecting or helping the other dream character.

Men's dreams more often than not take place outdoors in an unfamiliar setting. They usually involve physical activities, such as picking up objects, moving, bending, and talking to other dream characters.

One of the most striking differences between male and female dream reports is the number of references to travel. Whether it's by car, bus, plane, or boat, men make three times more references to traveling in their dreams than women do. Men also sleep less and, when they do dream, recent research shows that they report more incidences of pleasant dreams than women. Their pleasant dreams are usually about being on vacation, so it seems men like to use dreams to play. However, when men do dream about work, they are more likely than women to report stressful issues, such as being laid off and financial worries.

Men report more sexual interactions than women. When men dream of having sex, it tends to be with unknown women. Women are the opposite—in their erotic dreams, their dream self is usually coupled with their waking partner.

Women's dreams

In the normal dreams of women, about half of the other characters are known to the dreamer. Women mention significantly more family members and also more friends than men. Like men, though, the most commonly reported social interaction involves aggression, although it was more often verbal in the women's dream reports, involving arguments with another dream character. Aggression in the women's dreams usually involved male characters, as indeed did friendly interactions. The most common form of friendliness in women's dreams is helping or protecting others.

Women refer to more indoor and familiar settings, which are usually in their family home. The most common activities reported by women are moving or talking. Sexual dreams are less commonly reported. Women make more mention of emotions in their dreams, and as with male reports, when they do they were usually negative—predominantly fear and confusion.

Women's dreams are usually longer than men's, and contain far more detail, such as the color of objects or settings, and the facial features and clothing of other dream characters. Female dreamers are also much more likely to have conversations with others as they move around their dream settings.

Women's dreams tend to include more family members and friends than men's dreams. Women also dream more about familiar settings, such as the family home.

Common differences between the dreams of men & women

Dream research suggests that men and woman dream quite differently.

Men's dream content	Women's dream content
• More vacations	• Increasingly more about work
• More strangers	• More characters, especially family members
• More travel	• More familiar settings
• More aggression	• More emotion
• More sexual dreams, especially with unknown partners	• Sexual dreams, when they occur, tend to involve an existing partner

Sigmund Freud: The Unconscious Revealed

The work of Freud (1856–1939) on dreams has influenced all subsequent dream theory. His main premise was that "a remembered dream is a failed dream." He believed that the crude but necessary work of dreams is damaging to the conscious mind. A key concept in Freudian analysis is that dreams hold no spiritual, religious, or mythical significance.

Freud held a negative view of the basic nature of humankind. For him most of our waking behavior is determined by powerful innate forces or instincts. He believed there are two dominant instincts or libidos, namely eros (the life instinct) and thanatos (the death instinct), both of which are inextricably linked to the pleasure principle, which is the need we have to satisfy all our human urges. Of course, the social constraints we live with make this satisfaction impossible to achieve, and so we develop neuroses.

Freud believed that dreams allow our unsatisfied urges to be fulfilled outside waking consciousness, giving us wish fulfillment without any consequences. Our dreams satisfy our deepest wishes, however hidden within ourselves they may be.

Freud's view on dreams & human nature

To interpret dreams according to a Freudian perspective, it's important to understand Freud's view of the structures of personality and consciousness.

The structure of personality

- The *id* is the base part of our nature. It is instinctual and present at birth. The *id* is dominated by the pleasure principle and is animalistic.
- The *ego* is what we show the world. The ego develops from eight months onward. It tries at all times to be on good terms with the id and to satisfy its wishes, without making us look bad to other people.
- The *superego* is the part of us that has a sense of right and wrong—the "policeman" of the personality. The superego provides the id with constraints. This is our conscience at work.

The structure of consciousness

- *Consciousness* is what we are aware of. This is the tip of the iceberg: We are actually aware of very little of what is going on in our mind.
- *Preconscious mind* is the information that is just outside of consciousness but may become conscious. It is the buffer between unconsciousness and what we know, that is, what we are not currently aware of but can bring to mind.
- *The unconscious* is the biggest part of the mind. This is outside our awareness and cannot be brought into it. It is hidden and contains the vast majority of mental activity.

Manifest vs. latent content

According to Freud, manifest dream content is what we remember from a dream after we wake up. This is the surface of the dream and is what you would tell someone if you were to share your dream.

The latent content of the dream is hidden within the manifest content. Latent content includes unconscious wishes, emotions, fantasies, and conflicts, and it is only made accessible through analysis of the manifest content. The processes of hiding unconscious, unacceptable wishes in latent content and their transformation into manifest content is what Freud called dream work.

Free association

Freud recognized the importance of the symbolic content of dreams, arguing that symbols in dreams always have hidden meaning. He believed that this deeper meaning, which our conscious self would find distasteful, can only become clear through dream work. To understand our dream symbols, he developed a technique called free association.

Choose one symbol from a dream and allow yourself to think, write, or say anything that comes into your mind. Sit quietly and meditate on the symbol. Consider the symbol and your associations with it by focusing on:

- Its shape
- Its resemblance to other objects
- How you interact with the symbol
- Its resemblance to something else as suggested by its color

Together your answers will help you to understand the personal meaning of that particular symbol. Interpreting your dreams in this way, rather than simply assigning a set of symbols with a set of static meanings, is more likely to yield accurate results because it allows for your individuality as a dreamer.

What do Freud's symbols tell me about sexual fulfillment?

A less popular aspect of Freud's theory is his idea that many of our hidden wishes are related to sexual fulfillment. He eventually identified:

- 709 symbols that represent the penis
- 102 symbols that represent the vagina
- 55 symbols for sexual intercourse
- 25 symbols for masturbation

Some examples include: A gun for the penis and a purse for the vagina, plowing fields for sexual intercourse, and playing the piano for masturbation.

Freud argued that dreams deal with the animalistic aspects of human nature, which can be expressed through dreams.

Carl Jung: Connecting to the Universe through Dreams

Carl Jung (1875–1961) worked closely with Freud until they eventually became divided by the differences in their ideas about human nature and dreams. Jung's view of human nature and the purpose of dreams was more positive than Freud's. He introduced the idea, known as self-actualization, that each of us has an instinctual need to develop into the best human being that we can be. As a result, his work is known as positive psychology. Jung wrote extensively about dreams and made great efforts to put dream analysis on the therapeutic map; however, of the two, Freud is still known more widely for his work on dream interpretation. This may change as Jung's ideas gain more recognition.

To work with Jung's ideas, we need to understand his particular view of dreams and the structure of consciousness. He believed in individuality and maintained that each person should follow his or her own journey or path. He once said that, "The shoe that fits one person pinches another; there is no universal recipe for living." For Jung dream interpretation is specific to the dreamer. In fact he was the first person to propose that dreams serve more than one purpose.

For Jung every aspect of the dream represents a different part of the individual's psyche. Insects may play a positive or negative role in the dramas enacted in dreams. Bees and butterflies may have particular significance (see pages 49 and 50).

What is "active" imagination?

Jung called his methods for working with dreams "active imagination." The idea is to make the mind active and creative in its attempts to find a dream's meaning. Here are three active imagination techniques:

Amplification—Take a symbol, object, or character in the dream and identify as many different associations with it as possible.

Objective interpretation—Select an aspect of the dream that reflects an external aspect of your life, such as a person you know. This interpretation has personal meaning.

Subjective interpretation—In this process, you accept that every part of the dream reflects a subjective or internal state of you, the dreamer. When you dream, you enter a theater where you play out a story and act with various aspects of yourself. This interpretation often involves the use of archetypes.

The purpose of dreams

Jung identified two types of dream: Little dreams, which express the personal unconscious, and big dreams, which are linked to the collective unconscious. He identified several functions of dreams:

1. Dreams compensate for what it is we lack during our waking life. Neglected aspects of the personal unconscious, therefore, make an appearance in our dreams.
2. Dreams connect the dreamer with the collective unconscious. Jung believed that telepathy and precognition were possible through dreams.
3. Dreams have prospective power. Most dream interpretation techniques are retrospective (they help us understand our past). Jung's theory is prospective; he believed that dreams can give us hints of what the future holds.

Jungian techniques

One of the key features of a Jungian interpretation is that every aspect of the dream—the characters, the settings, the objects, the story—represents a part of the psyche. Each of these parts can be understood in terms of restoring psychological balance, because they help the dreamer to understand where he or she is in terms of psychological well-being; the different aspects of your dream represent the different aspects of yourself. Jung believed that every dream contains the following structure:

Jung's view on dreams & the structure of consciousness

The main difference between Freud and Jung is that Jung believed that dreams had spiritual potential. Jung believed that dreams could facilitate telepathy, that is, a dreamer's ability to read someone else's mind. He also believed some dreams are a form of precognition, which allow the dreamer to predict future events.

Jung's structure of consciousness

- *Consciousness* is what we are aware of.
- *The Personal Unconscious* is what we are unaware of but has been formed from personal experience.
- *The Collective Unconscious* is the part of us that goes beyond ourselves and joins the rest of humanity. The collective unconscious is inherited and is unaffected by personal experience. It is revealed through dreams containing symbols that express archetypes (see pages 38–57).

1. An opening scene that introduces the characters and setting. The dreamer may be in the kitchen, for example.
2. A main theme that will be revealed as the story develops. In this example the main theme could be that grandma is coming to visit and will bring cake.
3. A major conflict, for example, the dreamer cannot eat the cake because it contains insects but can't say anything because it might upset grandma.
4. An unfolding drama, as the main characters respond to the conflict. The dreamer takes a bite of the cake, but is then ill. Grandma shrieks, and the dreamer's mother enters the room...

Calvin Hall: The Continuity Principle

Hall believed that everything in our dreams can be interpreted, unlike Freud, who thought that dream meaning is hidden.

Seattle-born Calvin Hall (1909–1985) was a psychologist whose early work on dreams produced an archive of over 50,000 dream reports. He devised a system that divided dreams into categories, including settings, objects, characters, interactions, emotions, and misfortunes. His findings support Freud's idea of "day residue" in dreams, referring to the part of the dream that reflects waking experience. However, according to Hall, this is the part of the dream that we should use to make sense of what our dreams mean. His theory directly contradicts the idea that dream meaning is hidden (as Freud believed) and suggests instead that everything in a dream is interpretable in relation to our current or past waking life. He called this idea the continuity principle.

Hall based his opinions on evidence collected from large groups of dreamers, but he also analyzed "dream series" from individuals collected over a long period of time. A dream series is a large number of dreams recorded over time from one person. One of the series used by Hall contained 3,116 dreams recalled over 50 years.

What simple techniques can I use to analyze my dreams?

Hall made some helpful suggestions for analyzing dreams, and he didn't think you had to be an expert to uncover their meaning. To use his type of analysis, try the following techniques:

1. Record dreams as soon as you have them.

2. Record them on cards, so you can easily look through them and discover patterns.

3. Ask yourself:
   - Who was in the dream and what is their relation to you? List each character individually.
   - What takes place between you and these other characters?

Questions to ask yourself after you have recorded your dreams

Using Hall's ideas to understand your own dream life means accepting that your dreams can show you what you really think (rather than what it would please you to think) about the people, places, and roles you have in your lives, and those areas of your life where problems exist. Hall also compiled a list of questions to ask yourself after you have recorded your dream(s). The following are a selection that focus on other dream characters:

- Do I have frequent contact with the people in my dream in waking life? If so, what is the nature of this contact when I'm awake and how does it compare with my dream?
- Do any of the strangers in my dreams remind me of people I know in waking life?
- Does the dream contain people from my past? If so, have I thought about them recently? If not, is there any anniversary or reason why I would think about them now?
- Were any of the people I know distorted in some way? For example, was something wrong with their faces? What may be the reason for these distortions?

- Do I dream of children and babies? If so, what are they doing and how might this apply to a need that I have?
- What do my dreams tell me about my interactions with minority groups?
- What roles do members of the opposite sex take in my dreams? How might this apply to my feelings about them in waking life?

This is just a small sample of ideas that you could apply to the characters in your dreams. Your answers should link to your current waking life and help you identify concerns or outstanding issues you may have.

Case Study

Justine had a vivid dream in which she went to a conference to see a magician. Her father had died from a stroke not long before, and, although it now seems to her that the meaning of the dream is obvious, she needed to use Hall's techniques to realize the meaning for herself. The dream magician was paralyzed down the right side of his body and couldn't speak, but he approached Justine. She asked him if she was doing a good job with her life, and he reached out and held her hands. While he did this, she could hear him thinking that she was a good woman, and felt both comforted and rejuvenated. She couldn't explain why she woke up crying.

By asking herself Hall's questions, Justine realized that the magician character was her father, who had died suddenly without saying good-bye. Although her father had been very reserved and unaffectionate, the dream allowed her to see him through the eyes of the young girl she'd once been, as a magical man. Her dream confirmed what she had always known—that, despite his inability to ever say so, her father had loved her.

Fritz Perls: The Gestalt Interpretation of Dreams

Fritz Perls (1893–1970) developed the Gestalt method of therapy, and one of the most important parts of this was dream work. In Gestalt therapy the dream is "relived," and parts or all of it are played out using psychodrama techniques. Perls maintained that, "the whole is greater than the sum of its parts," by which he meant that our dreams contain parts of ourselves that we have disowned and need to reincorporate into the Gestalt (our whole selves). His method is one of the most original and holistic ways to work with dreams because you use images, feelings, sensations, or objects that are present in the dream, all of which are regarded as parts of you. According to Perls, everything in your dreams is in some way related to you, the dreamer.

You can use this method on your own or with a friend who is interested in working with dreams. Be warned: This approach is more suited to some people than others. To fully interpret dreams using Gestalt techniques, the dreamer may need to have a theatrical nature. There is no doubt, however, that the process of re-entering your dream can be a great deal of fun and extremely insightful.

The self is commonly represented in dreams by a mandala—circular, colorful, and symmetrical. The more complex the image, the more developed the dreamer's sense of self (see page 47).

Personality battle

Perls believed that a common conflict in dreams was a battle between the top dog and the under dog. The top dog represents the arrogant, aggressive, parental, or critical aspect of the personality; the under dog represents the victim, the whining, manipulative, and childlike part of the personality. Perls believed that balancing these two aspects in dream work led to resolution of being either all-knowing or immature in waking life.

How can I explore the layers of a dream?

The meaning of a dream can be as simple as the first impression it gives us, which may be its emotional tone or dominant image. However, we can extract meaning layer by layer to unravel the whole story. The case study on the opposite page can be used as an example. On first impression, it's a pleasant dream in which the dreamer meets the speaker at a work-related event. Less superficially, the dream concerns the dreamer's relationship with her father. At a deeper level it questions her relationship with herself and her need for her father's approval.

How to use Gestalt interpretation techniques

Perls's approach to dream interpretation asks that the dreamer re-enter the dream in order to explore which symbols correlate to his or her waking self. Playing out the dream can often lead to connections with our deeper feelings and our physical energies. Remember, the concept here is that each symbol in our dreams is part of ourselves. Use the following method to make your discoveries:

1. Tell your dream to someone or write it down, including as much detail as possible. Use the present tense.
2. After reporting the dream, take a few minutes to notice what stands out. It might be a scene, a character, or a feeling. As in the case study below, it could be the excitement of meeting celebrities.
3. The next stage is to become that part of the dream. So, in relation to the case-study dream, you would describe what it feels like to be famous. How does being a celebrity change you? What would your appearance be like and how would it differ from now? How does it feel?
4. Now it is time to create a dialogue between you and the part of the dream that stands out. A popular technique is the two chairs method. Position two chairs so that they face each other; choose one to represent you and the other to be the famous dream character; now have a conversation, alternating your position from chair to chair.
5. The final stage is to create an existential statement based on the conversation and dream work. The statement, in the present tense, should summarize the dream's basic theme and what it was trying to tell you.
6. Explore everything and ask yourself: If this were a part of me, what would it be?

Case Study

This case study gives an example of a positive dream, but Gestalt dream work can also be used to identify and resolve conflicts. Not long after his eighteenth birthday, Mark had a dream that he was at a party with a lot of celebrities. He was there with a close friend, whom he'd been thinking about vaguely during the day. The dream was very exciting. They couldn't believe who was in the room with them, and they were trying to get themselves introduced to the famous people.

When Mark told a family friend about the dream, she suggested they try the Gestalt method. He agreed, and, although he refused to take the process very seriously, he managed to come to a realization, which was, "I'm trying to meet the parts of myself that are exceptional and could make me famous!"

Perls believed that every dream captures an existential message or truth that we need to hear. These messages are communications from our unconscious minds, and, once we've heard them, they can be used to help us engage more fully in our lives.

Dream Interpretation:
An Eclectic Approach

An often overlooked aspect of dream theory is the emotional content of dreams. It is important to work with the whole dream experience to gain insight into your dreams.

Each of the dream theorists that we have featured has something to offer in respect to interpreting our dreams, but none provides the whole answer. Freud focuses on what is hidden in our dreams—that is, our base nature. Jung, being more hopeful, gives us a way to use our dreams for spiritual purposes and self-exploration. Hall's commonsense approach can work well with dreams that are obviously related to our waking lives, and Perls's ideas can be used in a more dynamic way to explore our dream content.

To benefit from their ideas, it is often best to take an eclectic approach to dream work. Eventually you will become proficient in all the different methods. It's important to remember that the overriding goal of dream work is to see the light. At this revelatory end point, a truth should be revealed to you that you were previously unaware of, which will tell you more about yourself or your current situation.

Emotional content

There is one great omission from the body of ideas that we have explored, namely attention to emotional content. Instead, symbols and visual images have been considered paramount in dream interpretation, even though both Jung and Perls accepted that every part of each dream is a part of the dreamer's self. We suggest that, as well as using the individual ideas of our featured psychologists, you focus on the emotional content of what you remember, and record it in relation to when it happens and with whom.

This approach allows you to work with one dream in isolation, or with a series of your dreams as you recall them over time. Patterns of emotion will start to reveal themselves over a period longer than 12 weeks. In Chapter 2, we look at what you are likely to remember and explain how best to keep a record. You will find that the same feelings recur in different contexts, and, while the same images and symbols may appear with these emotions, they will usually be distorted in some way from the original dream. The emotions, however, will remain the same.

What is my phenomenological journey?

Phenomenology is the term used to describe your experience of your own consciousness. This includes introspecting on your dreams in their entirety, not only what you visualized, but also what you perceived, felt, and experienced. As you embark on your unique journey, bear in mind these truths:

- Dreams are alerting you to the areas of your life that you can change for the better.

- Dreams will always tell you what these issues are if you carefully record what you can recall.

The role of our emotional selves

Recent positron emission tomographic (PET) scan studies of the brain during REM sleep reveal that the most active part of the brain in REM sleep is the amygdaloid complex, and not the visual cortex, as it was once supposed. The temporal lobe, which includes the amygdala, is the part of the brain involved with emotion and processing emotional memory. Scientists are, therefore, coming to the view that dreaming is a method of processing emotional concerns. In order to fully understand your dreams, you should consider and record how it felt to have the dream as well as the images, or story, the dream contains. This way you will work with the whole dream experience, not the pictures alone, and can make an individual analysis that is personal to you and no one else.

Try to see your dreams as messengers. They are alerting you to areas of your life that you can change for the better. They will always tell you what these issues are if you carefully record your dreams. Chapter 2 tells you in detail what you will remember in your dreams and how to record it. It will encourage you to bring dream work into your community. You will discover how to pay attention to all aspects of your dreams, especially the emotions they contain.

You can try many approaches in your dream work, always remembering that the ultimate goal is to reveal a truth about yourself that you had not known previously.

Catching Dreams

We know that the vast majority of dreams go unrecalled. What is it then about the other few dreams that makes them memorable for us? It could be that our ability to recall dreams is based on the time at which the dreams take place. We are more likely to remember the last dream we had because it is the one we experienced when we were closest to waking up. If we accept this explanation, the nature of the dream is unimportant in determining whether or not we recall it.

Another explanation is the "saliency principle." According to this, we remember dreams that are in some way outstanding. Therefore, we are more likely to remember dreams with strange or highly emotional content. However, this doesn't explain why we often recall dreams in which nothing much happens.

A third theory is that the dreams we remember are the ones that contain important information that can help us on our journey toward becoming a better, more whole, person. A dream like this may seem ordinary, and may be pleasant or disturbing, simple or complex, but the theory is that you have remembered it because it is important to your psychological development.

It is for you to decide which explanation suits your experience of dream recall. A 2008 report based on interviews with 93 men and 100 women in the U.K., showed that rates of dream recall vary, not only from person to person but also in the same individuals over time. One in two people reported a significant shift in the number of dreams recalled, compared to the number they used to recall. Some remembered fewer, and some remembered more, but the fact that recall varies is what is significant. More than 60 percent of the participants also said that the content of their dreams had altered, suggesting that it is not only how we remember but also the quality of dream experience that changes over a lifetime.

The ideal dream recaller

Research in the area of dream recall has shown that individuals with good recall have several factors in common. To achieve optimum recall, you will be someone who wakes up naturally, is well-rested, has an interest in dreams, and is motivated to record and pay attention to your dreams. You will also have a healthy level of stress and be facing some life issues that need to be resolved.

Schredl's four-factor model

Michael Schredl, a dream expert at the Central Institute of Mental Health in Mannheim, Germany, has identified four factors that affect whether we incorporate our waking lives into our dreams:

1. When the waking-life experience took place. If a waking-life experience is going to be incorporated into a dream at all, it will likely happen shortly after the event.
2. The dreamer's emotional attachment to the event that he or she is dreaming about.
3. The type of waking-life experience. It must be important to the dreamer.
4. The time of night. Our waking-life experiences are most likely to be included in the first two REM periods.

Rates of dream recall

On average people remember two or three dreams per week. The rate of dream recall varies across the lifespan—unsurprisingly younger people tend to remember more dreams than older people. Dream recall can also vary within each person; there will be times when recall is intense and times when it is sparse or nonexistent.

Case Study

Elizabeth, a 21-year-old student, woke remembering a strange dream. She had been in one of her housemate's bedrooms with her housemate and another friend. Then a close male friend had stormed in, announcing he had to marry them all. The friend said she couldn't because she was going to marry her boyfriend, but Elizabeth and her housemate laughed and accepted. They dressed in red and cream and went to church, but at the last minute, they changed their minds.

Why did Elizabeth remember this dream? It may be because she dreamed it just before waking up. Perhaps a conversation with her housemates or an incident the previous day was the trigger. The dream complies with the saliency principle because the content is both bizarre and emotionally charged. The other characters are ones Elizabeth is closely connected to in her waking life, and in this dream her unconscious mind is making efforts to process the intricacies of her relationships with them. As a female dreamer, she is also likely to be curious about her dreams and their meaning, which increases her probability of remembering them.

What Men & Women Recall

Women are usually more interested in their dreams than men. They pay more attention to their memories of dreams and share them with others.

Does being a man or woman have a bearing on whether we will remember a dream or not? We know already (see pages 10–11) that men and women have different types of dreams—or at least we know that there are differences in the dreams they remember.

However, to explore any difference in recall, dream researchers have to consider many factors. These factors may be intrinsic to being a man or a woman (intrapersonal factors, such as menstruation) or they may be more likely to affect men or women as they sleep and dream (interpersonal factors, such as work-related stress or tiredness).

Dreaming is generally believed to be a right-brain activity. The right side of the brain is often associated with anima aspects of personality: creativity, emotion, and unconventional thinking (see page 38 for an explanation of the anima archetype). The left side of the brain is more logical, mathematical, and driven by rules, and, therefore, associated with typically male characteristics. One thread that runs through research on dreams is that women are usually more interested in their dreams and, as a result, pay more attention to what they remember of their dreams and more often share their dreams with others.

Responses to the question "Has your dream recall changed over time?"

	Men (%)	Women (%)
I dream more than I used to	18	17
It's about the same	51	54
I remember fewer dreams	24	24
I remember dreams much less than I used to	8	5

The influence of the right brain

Interest in dreams is one of the most important factors in determining who remembers dreams and who does not. The fact that you are reading this book and reflecting on your own dream life may affect your dreams, their content, and the frequency with which you remember them. This is because you have brought your dream life into conscious awareness. Researchers have found many other factors that influence how frequently we are able to recall our dreams, as set out on below.

Factors associated with dream recall frequency

Men

Interpersonal factors

- Job-related stress can increase dream recall
- Consumption of alcohol can increase dream recall in the second half of the night
- Waking repeatedly during the night increases dream recall
- Overtiredness reduces dream recall
- Unnatural awakenings, such as interruption by an alarm clock, reduce dream recall
- Sleeping in a strange bed reduces dream recall

Intrapersonal factors

- Being susceptible to stress increases dream recall
- Physical illness increases dream recall
- Facing major life changes or significant challenges increases dream recall
- Having thin boundaries (being less able to shut out the world, life events, and their effects) increase recall

Women

Interpersonal factors

- Divorce or the end of a significant relationship can influence recall. Women who adapt well to these changes dream more frequently; those who adapt less well don't dream as much
- Family issues increase the rate of dream recall
- Working mothers dream less, probably due to tiredness

Intrapersonal factors

- Menstruation increases recall of aggressive dreams
- Women who register high scores in intuitiveness, introversion, contentiousness, and creativity recall a lot of dreams
- Having thin boundaries (being less able to shut out the world, life events, and their effects) increases recall
- Being creative increases dream recall
- Facing major life changes or challenges increases dream recall

Improving Your Rate
of Dream Recall

Some people say that they never remember their dreams. If you have difficulty with recall, then there is a range of methods you can use that will help.

The most important factor is a desire to remember. If you *want* to remember your dreams, and bring that desire into your waking consciousness, your rate of recall is bound to increase.

As a first step, try writing down a dream that you had in childhood, and then the last dream that you remember having. It doesn't matter how long ago these dreams occurred—just write them down in as much detail as you can remember. Ask yourself what is memorable about these dreams. Were they outstanding in some way? Focusing on past dreams will bring your mind's attention to dreams you are experiencing now.

What will improve my dream recall?

Physical and environmental factors can affect our dream recall. Take the following steps to ensure you are as ready as you can be for your dreams:

- Reduce, or ideally stop, drinking caffeine and alcohol.

- Don't go to bed on a full stomach.

- Don't exercise during the final hour before you go to bed.

- Burn clary sage (*Salvia sclarea*) oil in your bedroom for about an hour before going to bed. Take a long sniff just as you prepare for sleep. This herb is renowned for clearing the head and for producing vivid dreams.

- Make your bedroom the most welcoming room in the house. It should be where you feel most comfortable.

- View your bedroom as the place where you go to dream rather than to just sleep.

How to increase dream recall

In order to influence dream recall, you will need to make dreams a part of your daily routine—practice these steps to improve dream recall.

1. Think positively about your dreams. Make them an important part of your life. During the hustle and bustle of daily activity, take time to stop for a moment and ask yourself, "What will my dreams have to say about this situation later?"

2. Think differently about the dreams you have. In modern Western culture, we tend to think of dreams as single, isolated events that occur between two periods of waking, but the reality is that our dreams are connected across far longer periods of time. Over months of sleeping, the same emotions occur over and over again. The more we observe our dreams, the more we learn. You may discover that a dream you had three months ago has a connection with the dream that you had the previous night.

To improve dream recall, set aside 30 minutes every day when you can think about yourself and any changes you would like to make in your life.

3. Find 30 minutes every day to be with yourself, as far as possible free from any disturbances or distractions. Disconnect the phone, television, or anything else that could interrupt this time of reflection. Think about yourself, what you are happy with, and what you would like to change. The technical term for this process is "critical reflection." It is a form of focused consciousness that allows aspects of the unconscious mind to surface into preconsciousness and then into our dreams. Critical reflection should become part of your daily routine, and not only while you are trying to improve your dream recall. Once you realize what an oasis it provides in your busy daily life, you won't find it as difficult to find the time because you will naturally want to do it. It's your chance to think about and plan how to change your life and yourself for the better.

Keeping a Dream Journal

A dream journal is an essential tool in helping you to organize your dream work. If you approach the task with enthusiasm and commitment, you will be amply rewarded in terms of personal insights and development. Rather than being a record of your dreams, your journal will become more of a diary, which reflects your waking concerns and their manifestation in your unconscious.

Start by selecting a journal that you appreciate, which has special meaning to you. Place inside it mementos of personal importance, such as a photograph of yourself as a child, a flower you picked on a walk, a picture you have drawn, or something given to you by a loved one. Including this kind of memorabilia will help to make the journal special and give you an emotional link to it.

This is particularly important if you are a low recaller, or if you want to increase your dream recall, because the emotional investment you put into setting up the journal will open up the pathways between the part of your self that dreams and the conscious part that writes up a journal.

Preparing to record your dreams

The following activities will help you to jog your memory and increase your dream recall:

1. Write a brief history of your life and the outstanding events that have happened to you. Consider these memories as a story and ponder what type of story they would be.
2. Next, write about how you feel at the moment: What is happening in your life now? What are you happy about? What would you like to change about yourself or your situation?
3. Prepare to dream. During the daytime, think about dreaming and remembering your dreams after you have them.
4. Keep your journal close to you while you sleep so that, if you wake up, you can record your thoughts or memories.
5. Do your journal work on the weekend, or when you can wake naturally. Don't get out of bed immediately. Try to wake slowly and recall what is in your mind.

Recording your dreams in your journal

1. Write down everything that you can remember. Describe the setting, and whether it was familiar to you, or strange and unknown. Give a description of others in the dream, including their age, gender, and relationship to you. Note any animals or unknown characters. Most importantly, include how you felt during the dream, and whether or not this changed as events unfolded. Write the story from beginning to end. Finally, note down how you were feeling when you woke up.

2. Read the dream through. Have you forgotten anything? If so, add it.

3. What are your first impressions after reading? Write them down. Ask yourself if there is any obvious link to your waking life. If so, write it down.

4. What was strange in the dream? Did you do or say anything that wasn't typical of you? Ask yourself why this might have happened, and what it might mean.

5. Finally, in two columns write down what you understand from the dream and what you don't.

Throughout the day, reflect back on the dream. The 30 minutes of critical reflection you have put aside for yourself would be a good time to do this. Take this meditative time to think about what you don't understand about your dream. What has it left unresolved?

Recording your dream-life emotions

Using a simple chart will help you to pinpoint which emotions you felt at particular points in your dream. Fill in a chart for every dream you have, and you will soon notice patterns.

Dream	Emotion	Intensity 1–5*	With whom?	When
I was jumping through sand dunes with my friend. We could jump really far, like we were flying. We were jumping around, meeting our school friends.	Happiness Friendliness	4 4	A man that I have known for a long time, probably my best friend.	I felt happiness as we were jumping in the air, I felt free and exhilarated. I felt friendliness toward all the people I knew from school.

* 1 = very mild but present   5 = very intense

Incubating Dreams

American psychologist Julian Jaynes suggests that our ancestors believed that dreams were the voices of the gods and, therefore, acted on what their dreams directed them to do.

The practice of incubating dreams—encouraging certain types of dreams—is an ancient one. Temples built for this purpose have been found in ancient Egypt, China, and India. People want to stimulate dreams because they recognize that the dreaming mind is creative and can provide solutions or identify problems that are outside of our waking consciousness.

One type of dream that people have wanted to induce historically is a prodromal dream (see page 79). Prodromal dreams foretell physiological health or illness. In other examples of incubation, a request is made for a dream that will link the dreamer to the dead. Dreams are still used for divination or necromancy (speaking with the dead) in some indigenous cultures, such as the North American Blackfoot, Kwakiutl, Menomini, and Northern Iroquois peoples. In the U.K., too, a recent survey found that over 25 percent of Britons still believe it is possible to communicate with the dead via dreams.

The idea that we can direct our dreams rests on the assumption that dreams can guide us in ways that are not open to us in our waking lives, especially in solving problems or resolving issues. If you think it would be useful to have a particular dream, there are various steps you can take to incubate the dream.

How to give your dream a direction

The following instructions are based on the incubation method by Gayle Delaney, cofounder of the Delaney & Flowers Dream and Consultation Center in San Francisco. There are some additional suggestions that will help you to harness both the positive and negative aspects of your dreams.

- Identify the problem.
- Choose a night when you are not overtired or anxious and are generally feeling well and relaxed. Avoid caffeine and alcohol.
- Spend 5–10 minutes recording what has happened in your day, which aspects stood out, and how you are feeling now.
- Write down the problem in as much detail as possible: Who is involved and what is the exact nature of the issue for you? Which solutions have you tried? What do you see as the cause of the problem? How might you be an obstacle to solving it?

- Spend 15 minutes thinking about the issue from as many angles as possible. What do you see as the cause of the problem? If you can see a solution that you haven't already tried, consider why you haven't. How do you gain by having this issue in your life? For example, what would you have to give up if the problem were solved? What would change for you?
- Now write a *one-line* question that encompasses what you want your dream to show you. For example, "What can I do to change this behavior next time it happens?"
- Repeat this question to yourself as you go to sleep.
- Record everything you remember when you wake up.

Dreams are rarely altogether positive or unpleasant. It might help, therefore, to list the content of your dream in two columns. Use one column for the positive aspects, and the other for the unpleasant or apparently negative components. Both will tell you something about how to resolve the issue.

Look for the solution in the dream. Sometimes this may be obvious, but more often than not, the answer will be hidden in the metaphorical images that dreams contain. So choose your method of interpretation as outlined in Chapter 1 (see pages 12–21), and explore the possible answers that your dream has provided.

Case Study

PROBLEM I've been accepted at a medical school that is asking me to pay $500 to secure my place, and I have to make this payment before hearing back on my application from my top three medical school choices.

DREAM It was winter. I was receiving rejection letters from everywhere, so I decided to pay the $500.

The dream report above was collected during research carried out in 1993 by Deirdre Barrett. Barrett, who teaches at Harvard Medical School and Suffolk University and also works with dreams in private practice, asked 26 students to take part in a dream study to incubate the solution to a problem they had.

Over half the participants subsequently reported a dream that they felt was related to their problem. However, only a third of these dreams also included a solution, as in the example above. The conclusion of the study was that dreams are more likely to focus on a problem rather than a solution.

Inducing Lucid Dreams

A lucid dream is one in which you know you are dreaming. In most of our dreams, we have no awareness of being in a dream and we observe, or take part in, the dream events without questioning them. In a lucid dream, however, the dreamer's sense of agency is present; not only are we aware that we are dreaming, but we can also change the dream in ways that suit us.

How can I recognize lucid dreams?

The first person to write about lucid dreams was Fredrick van Eeden in 1896. He coined the term that has been used ever since.

- Lucid dreams are closely associated with experiencing out-of-body experiences (OBEs).

- Lucidity is more likely to occur in optional sleep (for example, sleep that results from napping on the weekends).

- Women report more lucid dreams that men. However, the researcher Jayne Gackenbach suggests that this is because women generally remember more dreams.

The lucid dream experience

Research on lucid dreams, conducted in Canada in 1987 at Athabasca University, found that they are almost always emotionally positive and can contain intense emotional experiences, such as awe or ecstasy. Quite often this type of dream is described as "transcendental" and results in the dreamer making changes in his or her waking life. Lucid dreams are also frequently regarded as otherworldly, especially because the lucid dreamer may believe that he or she is looking down on the planet from space, or flying around the world. Research has shown that people who have lucid dreams may be more likely to have out-of-body experiences (OBEs) during waking. Lucid dreams are often highly desired. This may be due to an unspoken belief that people who can dream lucidly are more spiritually or psychologically developed.

Step-by-step guide to lucid dreaming

Can we induce lucid dreams? The answer is an emphatic yes, but it may take practice. If you are currently working on increasing your recall of nonlucid dreams, it is best to become more proficient in this area before beginning exercises to induce lucidity.

1. Write a capital "C" on your nondominant hand. Every time that you see it during waking hours ask yourself "Am I dreaming?" With time, you will become so used to seeing the C on your hand, that it will be incorporated into a dream. You will then be prompted to ask yourself: "Am I dreaming?"

2. In the 30 minutes you put aside for yourself every day, spend 5 minutes sitting or lying quietly, and imagine the last dream you had. Feel what it was like in as much detail as possible. Then say: "This is what it feels like when I am dreaming." Consciously acknowledge this altered state of being.

3. During the day, as life events occur that are particularly emotional or unusual, ask yourself: "Is this a dream?"

4. If you have a recurring dream, think about it and repeat to yourself: "This is a dream." The next time you have the same dream, you will probably ask the same question and induce lucidity.

There are two common occurrences that you should be aware of when practicing. First, most dreams become lucid when the dreamer notices something slightly wrong in the dream. For example, she realizes that a light switch is in the wrong place. This incongruence is the prelucid phase of the dream and can induce lucidity. Second, when training yourself to be lucid, it is possible to wake yourself up with the shock of having managed it. Persevere: If you have gotten this far, lucidity is only a matter of time.

Lucid dreams are more likely to occur during optional sleep, for example, when napping on weekends.

Case Study

Here, Brenda (21 years of age) recalls a lucid dream in which she watched and supervised the creation of her ideal home.

"My dream began with me standing on an empty plot of land. As I was standing there, I imagined walls appearing on all sides of this empty plot. I slowly built a large mansion, with big wooden doors, a large front porch with white marble flooring, painted in off-white. Behind the big house was a large, beautiful garden with lots of flowers and rose bushes. Big trees appeared covering the back windows. I created a balcony to overlook fields that were planted with wheat and rice. As each detail of the house came into being, I became happier. If something was not going the way I wanted it, then I erased it! As the dream progressed, I started to add people to it: my parents and my brothers and sisters, and all my favorite celebrities. At the end, I stood back to admire my dream house, and I was ecstatic."

Children's Dreams

After observing unborn babies sleeping, dream experts concluded that humans spend almost 75 percent of total sleep time in the womb dreaming. A propensity for REM-type sleep carries through into life, and, in newborn babies, these rapid eye movements can be easily observed. In the first year of life, REM reduces slightly, to 66 percent of total sleep time, and by adulthood has settled at between 15 and 20 percent. This has led dream psychologists to conclude that REM is essential for brain development.

Are we born to dream?

The most famous study of children's dreams was conducted by psychologist David Foulkes in his sleep laboratories at the University of Wyoming and the Georgia Mental Health Institute in Atlanta. The study, which involved waking children from REM sleep to record their dreams, began in 1967 and continued until 1982. Foulkes's findings are presented in *Children's Dreams: Longitudinal Studies*, and although this book was written almost 30 years ago, it is still greatly influential.

Foulkes showed that children's ability to dream, or to report their dreams, develops in parallel with the cognitive abilities they demonstrate when they are awake. Younger children have fewer dreams, and their dreams are less complicated than the dreams of older children. Foulkes concluded that dreams develop in stages and that the content and topics of children's dreams can be categorized according to age.

Many of these research findings contradict folk beliefs about children's dreaming, because they highlight how mundane and unexciting most children's dreams are. Children are more likely to dream of indeterminate animals than witches or fairies. Foulkes's data, obtained from children between 3 and 15 years old, suggests that children get better at dreaming as they grow older. Eventually the child reaches a stage of psychological development at which their dreams become sophisticated stories that contain personal meaning. By then, the child is dreaming like an adult.

Should I pay attention to my children's dreams?

The common conclusion of Foulkes's, Adams's, and Valli's work is that the dreams of our children should be listened to and taken seriously. Children's dreams have not received as much interest from researchers as adult dreams, and yet their shifting content has important things to tell us about early development. The metamorphosis of a child's dream characters from animals to humans, for example, marks a key change in the child's relationship with the world. The fact that the humans are people that the child knows is also significant, because it shows that the child has started to reflect on his or her relationships during waking life.

What do children dream about as they progress through childhood?

Foulkes's findings, summarized below, show that the older a child is, the more likely he or she is to report being present in the dream, rather than only an observer of the action. From the age of five upward, children take an increasingly large part in their dream activities. Foulkes also discovered that the earliest childhood dreams contain only animal characters. As the child develops, the animals are gradually replaced by humans.

Age 3 and below Children do not normally recall dreams.

Ages 3–5 Dreams are static snapshots. Recall is still rare. The child is almost never present in the dream, but experiences it as if watching an external event. The characters are usually animals or fictitious creatures. The content of these dreams is mundane and void of emotion.

Ages 5–8 Dreams begin to include sequences of events and possibly more than one setting. The dreamer gradually begins to engage in the drama, although there is still only limited evidence of the child in the dream. Characters include humans as well as animals.

Ages 9–11 The dreamer and the dreams become more creative. Dreams during this period may contain a plot and be more filmlike.

Age 12 onward Dreams begin to take the form of adult dreams. The dreamer now shows an ability to be social and interact with others. He or she also demonstrates creativity and problem-solving skills. Most importantly, the dreamer can employ self-reflection by observing his or her own behavior, thoughts, and feelings in the dream. Some dreamers may begin to experience lucidity. Adolescence is also the peak period for flying dreams, although we don't know the reason for this.

What children's dreams can tell us

More recently, the spiritual awareness of children in relation to their dreams has been investigated by Dr. Kate Adams, a British researcher in education. Her work in 2005 and 2006 shows how children of all ages reflect their spiritual concerns when they relate their dreams. She concludes that we should listen to our children's dream reports because they may be trying to communicate their waking concerns. They may be exploring their perceptions of God, or considering the nature of friendships, their worries about the planet and global warming, or the extinction of an animal species. Because children's dreams can be important, they are often used to plan therapeutic interventions when a child has been traumatized.

Childhood dreams and dreaming are under-researched. Much of what we know about them is still based on Foulkes's study. Dr. Katja Valli at the University of Turku, Finland, recently presented findings that add to his work. She and her colleagues concluded that children have dynamic dreams earlier than Foulkes suggests. Valli found children under five who had dynamic dreams. Her research also suggests that consciousness is more developed in younger children than Foulkes thought. Younger children are better able to recognize themselves as separate from other people and to distinguish between the waking world and their dream one.

Children's dreams are important, because they may reflect their concerns during waking life.

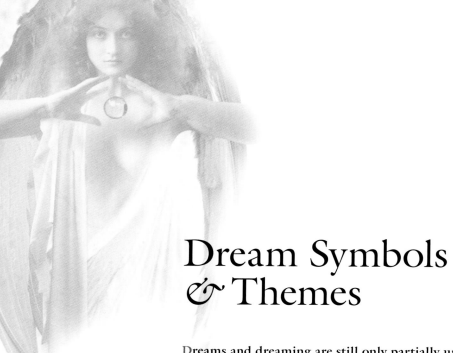

Dream Symbols
& Themes

Dreams and dreaming are still only partially understood.
As a result, dreams are often interpreted according to folklore
or personal opinion. Who hasn't shared a dream with a friend
and tried to pick apart its meaning?

Based on the research and analysis of prominent dream theorists,
this chapter brings together insights and interpretations of our
most frequently experienced dreams. In the final section, whole-
dream experiences, rather than just focusing on symbols or single
attributes of dreams, we explore particular types of dreams and
bring dream investigation up to the present moment. To enhance
your understanding of your dreams, suggestions are also included
to help you to put the interpretations to daily, practical use.

What Is Your Dream Telling You?

What do the symbols and themes in your dreams signify? Exploring each symbol, animal, place, or event in turn, this section will help you work through your own unconscious manifestations in your dreams and better understand the impulses behind them.

The Anima

The anima is an energy that represents everything we understand about the feminine. Views of what is "feminine" change over time and from dreamer to dreamer, so the anima archetype changes, too. She is linked to emotion, esthetics, art, softness, and creativity. She is usually female, and often beautiful, idealized, and voluptuous. The anima enjoys center stage, and all other aspects of the dream will tend to gravitate toward her. Her charms can be hard to resist!

How dream analysts interpret it Jung believed that one of the main functions of dreams is to restore balance in the life of the dreamer, whether in our external, "real" life or the life that goes on in our heads. The anima will make an appearance when there's an imbalance, to bring it to our attention. You may dream of the anima if you are berating yourself for being too emotional or—if the scales are tipping the other way—for being too calculating. In Jungian terms this is the equivalent of being too feminine or not feminine enough.

Pay close attention to your anima, and whether you are a woman or a man, you will discover your true views on women. Some beliefs may be unconscious and be made conscious through your anima dreams. As you grow older, your ideas on what it means to be female will change and so your anima may change. She may first appear as a stranger who mesmerizes you with her beauty, then as she becomes more mature, she may transform into a warm and inspirational teacher.

Which variations of the anima appear in your dreams?

The anima can take many different forms in your dream life. She personifies archetypal feminine qualities, so don't expect a rounded personality. She may come to you as a temptress, a virgin, mother, princess, wife, maid, old woman, or maybe the moon.

Questions to ask yourself If you have an anima dream, ask yourself the following:

1. What kind of femininity does my anima represent? Is it a maternal figure, or was the emphasis on her sexuality?
2. Are the feminine and masculine sides of my personality out of balance at the moment?
3. What are the positive features of my dream anima?
4. Am I lacking any of these positive attributes in my life? Do I need to nurture myself more? Or do I need more female friends, who will bring motherly gifts of nurture?
5. Is this dream about a powerful female figure in my life?

Symbolizes femininity, the mother, emotion

The Animus

The animus is the male equivalent of the anima—the masculine aspect of the psyche. This figure will appear in your dreams as the perfect male. What exactly a perfect male looks like will depend on your own gender and particular viewpoint, which again depends on the wider culture. This most masculine of males is often an adventurer, a hero, or a father. If there is a strong male presence or energy in the dream—if you are in a monastery, for example, or in the presence of an army—you know that the animus is present.

How dream analysts interpret it Being either too male or too female is not a good thing in Jungian terms, because it means the personality is out of balance. Jung approved if a female patient reported a dream in which she had sex with a gorgeous unknown male. He didn't believe dreams like this were about sex, but that they represented the perfect merging of both the male and female aspects of the dreamer's psyche.

Freud never used the term "anima," but he had plenty to say on the subject. He believed that a strong male presence in a dream showed unresolved issues with men in the dreamer's life. Dreams like this, therefore, may be alerting you to issues regarding your childhood relationship with your father, or your current intimate relationships.

Questions to ask yourself If the animus was present in your dream, ask yourself:

1. Which male characteristics do I value and admire?
2. Am I too feminine (in the traditional sense of that word)? Would it help me to be more masculine in some of my dealings with others?
3. How did I respond to the male characters in my dream?
4. Who was in control? Was it me or the other characters?

Symbolizes masculinity, the father, strength

How can the animus change form?

Dream therapist Carol D. Warner observed the animus in her dreams over a 17-month period. Her animus initially appeared as a strong African man who helped her to find her way. By the end of the recording period, most of the unknown men in her dreams had become competent, helpful, and assertive. In recognizing this, Warner realized that she had become more comfortable with the masculine aspects of her personality.

The Persona/Ego

Your persona is the face you show the world. It isn't the real you, but it's what you want other people to see. Like all archetypes, it will appear in dreams as a character other than you, the dreamer. The persona frequently takes the form of a larger-than-life character, literally and metaphorically, who behaves in a socially unacceptable way. A very dominant figure in a dream, for example, can represent the persona's tendency to override an individual's true nature. Many therapists believe that the persona's appearance indicates difficulties in being true to oneself. If you are crying on the inside, your persona may smile. If you are afraid, your persona may be fearless to the point of irresponsibility. Dreams that include this archetype are the attempts of your unconscious mind to process this kind of contradiction.

What is the function of the persona?

A normal persona is useful to us. It may be inappropriate to show how you really feel, especially if you assume a leadership role in your work. The persona also allows us to adopt an aspirational version of ourselves, which can lead to a change in our behavior. If the persona becomes inflated, it may appear often in dreams. Or this may be because of an unconscious drive for progress: Your mind urges you to attend to the masks you wear in order that you may become a more authentic person.

How dream analysts interpret it Jung believed that the persona is a mask that we put on to "face" the world. It is the stage character that we have chosen to play. Since most of us like to think well of ourselves and to have other people to do the same, our persona is usually a fairly wholesome construct. However, it is only a construct and not the whole story. Jung believed that if you dream about your persona, you need help to find your true self. As you become truer to your self in your waking life, your persona will change form in your dreams. For example, a persona that takes the form of a clown, signifying the dreamer's use of humor to deflect emotion, may eventually become the circus master, when the dreamer has learned to take charge of his or her feelings.

Questions to ask yourself If you dream about the persona, ask yourself the following:
1. Who am I trying to impress and why?
2. Do I know who I am, or is my life superficial in some areas?
3. What would happen if I showed people my true self? Would it be as bad as I think?
4. Which parts of my public face allow me to survive situations that I find difficult?

Symbolizes acting, masks, misperception, superficiality

The Goddess

The goddess is a highly regarded dream symbol. She is the manifestation of feminine goodness that lies within us all. Her appearance in dreams is a blessing. She takes different forms, according to the dreamer's cultural or religious leanings, but her superhuman powers distinguish her from the anima. The goddess may also appear in our dreams as someone we consider to be above us on account of her goodness and mercy. In Western society many followers of new-age religions seek to wake the goddess or reintegrate with this part of themselves. In symbolic language she is referred to as the mother and nurturer of both the psyche and humanity as a whole. The powerful energy of the goddess may visit your dreams as the moon.

How dream analysts interpret it Jung believed that there is a perfect person within each of us. It is our life's journey to bring perfection into our waking life and realize our potential. In these terms the goddess represents our fundamental human need for spiritual growth and perfection. Her appearance in a dream reawakens our drive toward this symbolic ideal. This is why dreaming of the goddess is often a life-changing experience.

The goddess enjoys widespread popularity as a social archetype. Her presence can be seen in women's successful attempts to influence the external world, at work and within the family. The English journalist Tony Crisp suggests that when we dream of the goddess, we dream of our unconscious connection to all women. He points to the qualities that make women mysterious in the eyes of men and the influence of the moon. A waxing half moon indicates the premenstrual, developing female. A full moon is a woman in her prime. A waning half moon in a dream indicates a postmenopausal woman. The three symbols together show the goddess in her totality.

Questions to ask yourself To make the most of this special dream symbol, ask yourself:
1. Which parts of me yearn for the heavenly or divine?
2. How did I feel after this dream? Was it transformative?
3. Could the goddess be someone I know in my waking life?
4. What did this dream add to my existence?

Symbolizes perfection, extraordinary abilities

What can goddesses represent?

Goddesses in mythology can teach you about the meaning of your dreams. Athena brings wisdom and may stand under an olive tree or appear with an owl. Aphrodite, the goddess of love, often appears with a dove. Demeter brings fertility and may hold a scepter or a torch. Hera, the goddess of marriage, wears peacock feathers. Hestia, the goddess of the home, stands next to a hearth or an open fire. The more you research these powerful figures, the more likely they are to bring their qualities to your dreams.

The Rescuer

This is not an easy symbol to interpret, and it may take many forms. The context is crucial to its meaning. The dreamer may rescue others, or others may rescue the dreamer. Sometimes, the rescuer takes the form of the emergency services—police, firefighters, physicians, or ambulance crews—indicating that the dreamer is overwhelmed by his or her responsibilities. One common manifestation of the rescuer is as a friend on the telephone, who is helping the dreamer. This rescuer does not appear physically in the dream, but influences the outcome.

How dream analysts interpret it The rescuer is the part of the psyche that is energized when all feels lost. Jung pictured the human soul as a flame that can be seen in the dark. The flame is eternal, because nothing, no matter how bad, can extinguish the soul. The rescuer, therefore, is the part of everyone that provides strength and support, usually in times of crisis. A rescuer may even sacrifice his or her own life to save another character in the dream, or because it would help the dream situation. Do you sense danger in your life? The rescuer in your dream may be an intuitive voice, alerting you to the problems you face. People who have experienced a particularly difficult life or many obstacles to happiness often forget that they can save themselves from harm. Clarissa Pinkola Estés, author of *Women Who Run With the Wolves*, talks about the gifts of the abandoned child and names the rescuer among them. This symbol may appear in your dreams to remind you that you don't have to wait for someone else to take action.

What is the function of the rescuer?

The rescuer brings both care and kindness to us in dreams. To honor this dream during waking, the dreamer needs to nurture him or herself. Many people want someone to rescue them in waking life, and they hand over the responsibility for their happiness to others. Dreaming of the rescuer reminds us that we can save no one but ourselves, and that the responsibility for this is ours alone.

Questions to ask yourself The rescuer in dreams often saves another dream character and, in doing so, pays a personal cost. Take a gestalt approach to a dream of this kind and ask yourself:

1. Which part of me is the rescuer?
2. Which part of me needs to be rescued?
3. Why and how is this relevant to my life now?

When you have answered these questions, make a waking rescue plan for the part of yourself that is communicating with you in this dream. Your plan must involve action.

Symbolizes altruism, unselfishness, rescuing the self

The Hero/Heroine

The rescuer tries but often fails, but the hero and heroine always save the day. In myth and legend, the classical idea of a hero is a character of either noble ancestry or very humble beginnings, who has great courage and strength, is bold in his exploits, and is the favored person of the realm. Modern heroes and heroines more often appear in forms that are influenced by the media or cultural icons. However you envisage your heroes and heroines, they will typically face great trials and forfeit everything to overcome the obstacles in their way. Fortunately, because it's a story with a hero, this dream will turn out well in the end.

How dream analysts interpret it The inclusion of this symbol in a dream is very powerful and suggests that the true self is making an appearance. Often the hero will have to travel to the underworld (the unconscious) to take on fierce creatures and overcome trials. This journey can be seen as an initiation the dreamer must undergo before accepting his or her true position in life. It is the hero's preparation before finally accepting his glory and the prize of becoming a well-rounded, fulfilled human being. But if your hero or heroine is disdainful or arrogant, Freud would say your ego needs to be examined. Now is the time to address the spikier parts of your personality during your waking life. Have you developed a superior attitude, for example, that manifests itself as arrogance or impatience with others? Do you secretly believe you are better than other people? In common with all the dream symbols, there is a negative and a positive side. In therapeutic terms, however, even an unattractive hero can teach us something.

Questions to ask yourself If the hero/heroine appears in your dream, ask yourself:
1. Which parts of me do I consider to be extraordinary?
2. How can I nurture these aspects of myself?
3. Do I have enough humility?
4. In the 30 minutes you set aside each day, meditate on the equality of all men and women.

Symbolizes overcoming obstacles, great courage, the part of the self that is extraordinary

A real-life heroine?

In a study of people who had dreamed about Diana, Princess of Wales (1961–1997), conducted after her death, Diana was often referred to as a heroine. Her role in dreams usually required extreme bravery. The study concluded that the princess has become a cultural symbol of the heroine archetype. The media has transmitted to our unconscious the idea of her as a heroine and so, when we need a heroine in our dreams, we may draw on her image. Your unconscious may find its version of a hero in a movie star or political figure.

Angels

Dreaming of angels is one of the most positive dream experiences we can have. These celestial messengers may appear in many forms, but they always suggest transcendence and the opening up of communication. You may dream, for example, of one of the four archangels of Christianity: Michael, Gabriel, Uriel, and Raphael. Each of these archangels has a different significance or attribute, and, if they appear in your dream, they may carry symbolic objects, such as flaming swords, musical instruments, or flowers. Angels may also appear in the form of androgynous, mystical characters.

How do angels appear in dreams?

Robert Van de Castle, author of *The Big Book of Angels* and one of the most significant contributors to dream research in the last century, has found that angels appear in dreams in several predictable ways. First, they often shape-shift from one character to another. Second, they are the most salient part of the dream. And third, angels are almost always part of positive dreams.

How dream analysts interpret it With rare exceptions, an angel appears in your dream with the express purpose of delivering a message. The angels are on your side, so the message will be a helpful one, and it will reveal to you some means to move forward in your life and transcend your current state of being. Jung believed that angels were intermediaries between lower and higher aspects of the self. Your angel spells out to you in a dream what at some level you already know or have been moving toward for a while. Jung also believed in the paranormal. Could your angel be a visitor from the divine?

Freud saw angels as a manifestation of the dreamer's superego, which is the part of us that believes we are mystical. To Freud, a female angel would represent womanly perfection. In a few cases a dream angel can have a metaphorical meaning. There may be people in your life that you think of as angels, and so they will appear to you as angels in your dreams. Consider your angel carefully to check it isn't a friend in disguise.

Try this to gain insight Focus on a single angel over the course of a week or for a given period of time. Bring the qualities of that angel to your mind during the day, then call the angel to you about 15 minutes before you expect to sleep. Developing incubation rituals can help the process; lighting a candle or some incense, for example, or meditating on the specific problem you would like the angel to help you with. In Jungian terms you are calling to the divine that is within us all.

Symbolizes communication, transcendence, spirituality

The Old Woman

This symbol is one of the most useful to work with in terms of self-development. The old woman is the seer, perhaps an elder, and the wisest of all women. She has learned through experience and wants to pass her wisdom on to the dreamer. Since one of her roles is to pass her womanly knowledge down to younger females, the wise old woman is linked to female rites of passage. She may appear as menstruation begins, during pregnancy, or as menopause approaches. The old woman almost certainly made more frequent dream appearances in the past, when it was more usual for women to live together in groups.

Groups of cohabiting females still exist, of course. In this context, the old woman is likely to represent intuition. People who cohabit also share their dreams, using them to understand each other and show support in their waking relationships. You may say to your housemate, for example, "I dreamed you got that job!" or "In my dream you looked so happy!"

How dream analysts interpret it This character is the most mature aspect of woman. Jung saw the wise old woman as the anima in her most evolved state. When she appears in a dream, she personifies female knowledge in magnificent amounts. To have access to this part of the self, a young woman (or a young psyche) may need to dig deep, but once contact has been made, she can be enormously helpful. For instance, the wise old woman may encourage the dreamer to exercise prudence.

Try this to gain insight The old woman is the key to your inner wisdom. Working with this archetype is very healing and can be a lot of fun. It can be especially comforting if you have never known your grandparents.

1. Take two chairs and place them facing each other.
2. Sit in one chair and talk to the old woman.
3. Tell her what is troubling you and ask her what to do.
4. Move to the other chair and be the old woman. Tell yourself what you should do. Be prepared to hear things that you don't want to hear. The old woman is honest, forthright, and has only your best interests at heart, so she will tell you the truth.

Symbolizes wisdom, healing, female rites of passage

How does age appear in dreams?

The characters that appear in our dreams can be younger than us, the same age as us, or older. Most commonly, they are the same age as the dreamer. Children and older adults appear less frequently. Older adults in dreams are usually grandparents or well-regarded aunts and uncles. Their presence is usually reassuring.

Children

Children are common characters in dreams and appear in various stages of their development. The newborn represents an idea that is unformed or undeveloped. This may refer to your relationship with yourself, or to a new venture or a project that you are working on in your waking life. A toddler can represent the way we stumble as we strive to develop, whereas a child of seven or eight epitomizes the state of childhood generally. Sometimes, a child appears in a dream as a projection of the dreamer's own needs. Children are widely perceived as innocent and free, and people often look on childhood as an idyllic time. A dream of children may represent a longing for the old days or a need to return to a less socially controlled version of ourselves.

How dream analysts interpret it In Jungian theory a child is a symbol of potential. The child represents an infusion of new blood. However, while children may appear as positive symbols, such as the magical child (abilities we are developing), the divine child (an emerging spirituality), or a child of nature (a love of the natural world), they can also appear in a more vulnerable form, representing aspects of our lives that, during waking hours, need to be honored. The orphan, the wounded child, or the eternal child will all appear to you in need of help. These children bring areas of our personality to light that are, as yet, works in progress.

Dreams of children should be placed in the context of our waking lives. Pregnant women often dream of the baby they are carrying. In these dreams it is normal for the baby to appear deformed, very big, or very small. Expectant fathers also have dreams of this kind. Parents may dream of a child having an accident. These dreams directly reflect waking concerns, which the mind plays out during sleep.

Questions to ask yourself If a child appears in your dreams and it is hurt or crying, ask yourself the following questions:
1. Which part of me is this?
2. What does the child want?
3. How would I take care of this child if it were mine?
4. Take your answer from question 3 and take action in your waking life, in whatever form is appropriate.

Symbolizes potential, new ideas, regression

Can dreams rescue our inner child?

Dreams can link to "inner-child" work, in which you address the dream child as if it were yourself at that age. Most people have issues from childhood, such as having felt unloved or abandoned by someone. It helps your adult self to work through these issues. When you set out to rescue your inner child, your dreams can tell you what to put right. When we act in waking life to reclaim this part of ourselves, the dreams of children stop. This shows that the work has been successful.

The Self

The self represents wholeness. The self will appear as a symbol rather than another character. The most common example is the mandala. A mandala is circular and usually extremely colorful and symmetrical, showing balance in every aspect. The mandala will be a central image in the dream, and it may appear as a lotus-shaped flower. It may also appear as any circular object that draws the dreamer's eye. The more complex the circular image, the more developed the person's sense of self will be. The mandala can symbolize the wholeness of the self. If it is broken, this represents an imbalance or a break of some kind in the dreamer's psyche. The dream shows your current state of development, without the distractions of the persona or ego.

How dream analysts interpret it Jung described the mandala as "a representation of the unconscious self." Unlike our conscious self, it is balanced and represents the north, south, east, and west, the above and the below. It has a core and a boundary. This symmetry is how Jung viewed the natural landscape of the mind. Jung also believed that the colors that make up each person's dream mandala can be interpreted in order to fully see the self. Achieving the balance represented by the mandala is at the core of Jungian dream work. If you know what your mandala looks like, then you know who you truly are.

Try this to gain insight Did you use a set of compasses to draw circles when you were a child? You can draw your own mandala in the same way. You are guaranteed to emerge from the exercise with a greater sense of completeness.

1. First allow yourself to re-enter the dream in which the mandala appeared. If you have not had this dream, spend time meditating and bring your mandala to mind.
2. Focus on the intricacies of your mandala. Examine the colors, shapes, and patterns that make it unique to you.
3. Do you notice anything of particular interest? If so, make a quick sketch or jot down some notes.
4. Once you have a clear vision of your mandala, spend time re-creating the image, using paints or other media.

Symbolizes the self, the true nature of who we are (as opposed to the persona, see page 40)

Why should I draw mandalas?

Every part of your dream mandala is informed by different parts of yourself. Jung used to draw his mandala regularly, and a selection was published in his great work, *The Red Book*. Jung believed that we are each set on a path to be the best person we can be. We can explore who this person is using creativity. This is why Jung advocated drawing mandalas and why his use of images and symbols is so pronounced in his approach to psychology.

Animals & Animal Deities

Animals in dreams often represent archetypal characters (see pages 38–47) in the form that they take at the start of the individuation journey, or at the beginning of a phase of personal growth. Animals reflect the untamed or raw aspect of archetypes before they are actively worked with during waking. As you begin to understand your dreams and yourself better, a fox in a dream may reveal itself as a wily or cunning human. Some animals have always been associated with spiritual significance and are revered in Hindu and Shamanistic cultures, for example. People who follow these traditions draw upon the strength of animal deities to improve on the frailness of their human capabilities.

How dream analysts interpret it It is vital to distinguish between animals and animal deities in your dreams. Animals can have either negative or positive meanings, depending on our associations with them. An animal deity, on the other hand, can represent a quality in you that you didn't know you had, which is currently only developed enough to assume an animal form. You may project one of your characteristics or attributes onto a dream animal that you are currently unable to own, or for which you don't want to take responsibility. Perhaps you are angry with someone close to you, but you are unable to express that anger for fear of losing that person. You might dream of a raging, ferocious tiger. Or you might feel hurt but be unable to acknowledge that pain in waking life. Then you might dream of a wounded animal.

Try this to gain insight We use an animal's essential attributes or energy to help develop a sense of who we are.
1. Is there a recurring animal in your dreams? If not, think of an animal you identify with in some way. It may be ferocious or unfriendly, but you can still work with it.
2. Make friends with your animal. Consider its attributes and how they relate to your own. Do you share this animal's characteristics or do you wish you did? Honor the animal in your dreams by donating to a charity that supports it.

Symbolizes extraordinary intuition and capabilities, emotions

How can I learn more about dream animals?

Look for stories or myths about any animals that appear in your dreams. If you dream of a whale, for example, look up the Bible story of Jonah. The whale helped Jonah, which suggests that the dreamer has the ability to show mercy. In fairy tales, the body of a whale often forms mythical islands, while the whale sleeps for centuries in the sea. This symbolizes the part of consciousness to which we have access, and the huge, uncharted unconscious that lies beneath the surface.

Bees

If bees feature in a dream, they usually make only a peripheral appearance. They may buzz around the flowers of a garden. Take a moment to think about bees: They live in colonies; They are one of the most socially organized of all creatures; And they are unwavering in their endeavors to keep the hive from harm. Each bee has its own duties, and it works all day to carry them out. If one of these creatures is buzzing around your head, examine it carefully. It may hold the solution to the problem (or what Jung called the drama) being played out in the dream.

How dream analysts interpret it Jung believed we have two types of unconscious mind: the personal and the collective. Bees, which have to be sociable to live, belong to the collective—the bee supports the idea that everything is running smoothly to bring harmony to the whole—and their presence may be a good sign. A lone bee, on the other hand, may indicate a need for support, or to become involved in a collective group or project. The precise meaning of your dream depends on where you are on your personal journey toward wholeness. Jung used the term "individuation" to describe this journey, which should develop over a person's lifespan. Freud interpreted the appearance of bees in dreams as a sign of neurosis, so they might be an irritating or even frightening presence. Alternatively, you may dream of bees because you lack clear social structures in your life. A first time away from home can engender feelings of this type. Although you may enjoy new freedoms, your unconscious mind may wish for the outer restraints provided by social rules and structures.

Try this to gain insight The key to dream analysis is to make the symbols work for you. To make use of what the bee is bringing to your dream, try the following exercise:

1. Think of a problem you have in current waking life and write it in your journal.
2. Which of the bee's qualities might lessen the problem?
3. Ask yourself whether you are the head bee or one of the workers. Is your position in daily life similar to the position of the bee? If not, does the bee represent an aspiration? Do you want more responsibility, or less?

Symbolizes immortality, health, unity, hope

What is the significance of nectar?

Nectar is referred to as the drink of the gods. The word derives from the Greek: *nek* means "overcoming" and *tar* means "death." To consume nectar is like imbibing a gift of ageless immortality, which can be viewed as a metaphor for psychological health. If the dreamer is physically ill, drinking nectar or eating honey may symbolize a turning point in the illness. In this sense the dream reflects changes in the body that the dreamer is, as yet, unaware of.

Butterflies

Myths about the butterfly may lie behind the old wives' tale that if we die in a dream, we will die in real life. Several societies in China and Japan believe that the butterfly is the vehicle used by the human soul when we sleep, and that it travels far and wide on our behalf. If the dreamer's sleep is interrupted—that is, if the dreamer is woken before the butterfly has returned—he or she will die because the soul is lost. The butterfly's life cycle is key to understanding the symbol in a dream. This fragile creature begins life as a caterpillar, then hibernates as a chrysalis before emerging as a beautiful butterfly. In its adult state it lives for only a short time, before fulfilling its instinct to lay eggs and repeat the cycle. The butterfly in a dream can, therefore, be treated as a metaphor for the natural cycle of transformation every human goes through during a lifetime.

How do butterflies reflect the dream experience?

One of the most famous dreams of a butterfly was recorded by Chuang Tzu, a Chinese philosopher (c. 370–301 B.C.). Chuang Tzu dreamed he was a butterfly, flying around and landing on the flowers. In his dream he didn't know he was Chuang Tzu. When he woke up, however, he knew he was himself. This story describes how dreams relate to our level of absorption and lack of reflectivity. Our total immersion can make it difficult to distinguish our dreaming experience from reality.

How dream analysts interpret it A dream of butterflies often carries a message of hope. There are times when we feel stagnant, when nothing seems to be changing in our lives or within ourselves. However, the greatest changes can emerge from dormant periods. Take the chrysalis as an example. To all intents and purposes it appears dead, but eventually it breaks open to reveal a glorious surprise. The message of the butterfly is that good things come to those who wait. The butterfly has a pleasing symmetry. Its wings reflect each other in shape, pattern, and color. A butterfly dream may refer to a period of rest, which enables you to restore your balance or equilibrium. This is valuable period of preparation for the changes you face ahead.

Questions to ask yourself Animals or insects in our dreams can signify people that we know. The butterfly may represent someone who is caught up in his or her personal appearance, or someone who has yet to learn that physical, youthful beauty is transient. This person may also flit from place to place and prefer not to settle anywhere. If your dream focuses on a butterfly or another variety of insect, ask yourself the following:

1. Do I know anyone like this?
2. If so, what is this dream trying to tell me about this person?

Symbolizes transformation, natural cycle of life, patience

The Bear

The appearance of the bear is a symbol of courage and is one of the most powerful of dream symbols. The bear survives in hostile territory, and when it cannot sustain itself during the harsh winter, it sleeps. This retreat can be seen as representative of the emotional hibernation that some people go through when they face a life challenge that is too much for them. The bear takes over until the person is ready to face the challenge, and also gives him or her the courage to fight. If you are in trouble, the bear is there to help.

How dream analysts interpret it The bear, with its long history, symbolizes the ancient side of our nature. It is that instinctual part of us that is untamed and wild. If the bear appears in your dreams, ask yourself what it is bringing to help you. The dream consultant Judith Picone writes in the journal *The Dream Network* that she uses a polar bear she once dreamed of to relax in her waking life, by walking and swimming with it in meditation.

This most caring of creatures shows great parenting skills. The appearance of a female bear in a dream may, therefore, suggest a need for mothering that was not met during childhood. If you dream that you become a bear yourself, your unconscious is telling you that you are now strong enough to confront a threat. When the bear appears in archetypal form like this, it is what Jung called a "big" dream. Whereas a little dream is usually linked to the personal unconscious or to daily life, a big dream is one of great significance for the dreamer and his or her future psychological development. As the bear, you are ready for any challenges you face.

Questions to ask yourself If you dream of a bear, ask:
1. Am I someone my friends can talk to about their problems?
2. Do I have the power to heal through my friendships and other relationships?
3. Who in my life needs me to listen to them?

Symbolizes courage, instinctual drive to survive, emotional hibernation

How can a bear represent power?

In this dream a young woman took on the form of a small grizzly. She understood that her name was Small Bear. A man was chasing her and he changed into a wolf, intent on catching her, his prey. The dominant emotion for the dreamer was terror, but the appearance of the bear changed this. The dreamer stopped running, turned to face the wolf, and repeated "small bear." With each repetition the wolf became weaker. This dream helped to transform the dreamer's view of herself, and with it, her life.

The Cat

If you look up the cat in a typical dream dictionary, you may find that it is a symbol of bad luck or ill fortune. That's not the whole story, so don't be disheartened if you dream of a cat. Like all dream symbols, the cat has positive aspects, too. What the cat is doing in your dream is vital to your interpretation. Exploring the cat as a dream symbol is also an opportunity to look at male and female behaviors, and how you conform, or not, to these. The tomcat is a wanderer and an opportunist. He does what he has to do, takes what he needs, and leaves. The female cat is content to sit in front of the fire and is also a fantastic mother. Both clear the house of vermin, which in the language of dreams equates to ridding oneself of negative thinking. Pay attention to your dream and no matter how mischievous your cat may be, she will be an aid to positive thinking.

Is the cat a survivor?

Many interpretations of cats in dreams focus on sensuality. However, the cat has many talents. She is also a survivor. If you have suffered a severe setback, whether a physical accident or an assault on your psychological well-being, the cat in your dreams can bring hope. Like the cat with its nine lives, you can learn to live again.

How dream analysts interpret it The cat is one of a series of animals, including the wolf, the bat, and the owl, that are associated with powerful, mystical, female energy. They are known as familiars and are believed to possess magical powers, or to enhance the feminine powers of their owner. In Jungian psychology the cat is the epitome of feminine magic. A dream of a cat may be an intense experience. Barbara Hannah, who has written about Jung's lectures on animals, links the cat in dreams to independence, resilience, and motherliness. Freud also saw the cat as a symbol of femininity. He said, "Time spent with cats is never wasted," and we can assume that he felt that time spent with women was never wasted either. He believed that the cat in dreams embodied feminine desires and impulses. What was the cat doing in your dream? Its behavior can reveal the state of your sexual self and how at ease you are with your sexuality.

Questions to ask yourself You can use the cat to start an internal conversation. Start by exploring cat-related sayings:
- "Every time something bad happens, she lands on her feet." Can this be said of you, or anyone that you know?
- "Curiosity killed the cat." What or whose business are you in that isn't good for you?

Symbolizes the feminine, sensuality, female genitalia, positive thinking

The Dog

Along with the cat, the dog is the most common of domesticated pets. And like the cat, as a dream symbol it has strong links to sexual energy. The difference is that the dog, as man's best friend, is generally held to be more wholesome. The dog symbolizes loyalty, trust, and unconditional friendship. If you dream that you are a dog, it may reflect your ability and willingness to serve a master, whomever or whatever that master may be. Because it is such a positive symbol, with happy connotations, you are likely to wake from any dream of the dog wanting more from the experience. You can use this energy usefully to take the qualities of the dog into your waking life.

How dream analysts interpret it The meaning of a dog in your dream may take some time to unravel. There is the side of us that is loyal and wants to belong to the pack. There is also the side that is competitive, who wants to be top dog. What breed of dog were you in your dream? A dream of a poodle has different connotations from a dream about a Doberman. Whereas a dream of poodle would indicate concern with outward appearance, a Doberman is linked to aggression. A lowly position in the pack suggests a sense of inferiority. If you feel undervalued in your daily life, you will generate neurotic energy, which will use your dream symbols to find expression.

Questions to ask yourself To work with the dog in your dream, ask the following questions. These work equally well with the cat symbol.

1. Are you a cat or a dog person? Why?
2. Consider the dog in your dream. If you were that dog, what would you need to do for yourself?
3. If you were to encounter the dog that was in your dream in waking life, how would you treat it? How does this relate to the way that you treat yourself?

Symbolizes loyalty, trust, and unconditional friendship

What if an animal in my dream has human qualities?

If your dream dog can talk, or shows any other human capabilities, it means that you are moving from one stage of development to another. A dream in which you give a dog a command and it says "no," for example, demonstrates both another quality of the dog, disobedience, coupled with a progression—the human ability to talk. It shows that the dreamer is developing the ability to refuse requests in cases where he or she had previously said yes without thinking.

The Wolf

The wolf is a wild animal that can be savage and dangerous. A dream of one, if not a nightmare, is likely to have an edge. However, wolves are also devoted mothers. It can help to be fierce when you need to protect your young. A she-wolf will even feed the cubs of other wolves, if necessary. As with all dream symbols, you can interpret the wolf from many angles. In ancient times wolves were believed to carry the souls of the dead they had eaten inside their bodies. With this in mind, you may discover your dream has links to reincarnation.

No discussion of the wolf could pass without mention of the werewolf. This mythical creature is a common feature in children's dreams. At a 2009 conference of the International Association for the Study of Dreams in Sweden, researcher Dr. Katja Valli presented findings suggesting that children of the age of about eight or nine dream of animals transforming into people (see also pages 34–35). Dreams of werewolves, then, may be the result of this dramatic developmental stage.

What shows the wolf as a protector?

The Berserkers were ancient Norse warriors, whose apparent uncontrolled rage during battle is recorded in numerous Old Norse sagas and poems. They wore wolf or bear pelts instead of armor in the belief that this gave them the strength and attributes of a wild animal. Likewise, prehistoric Irish tribes wore wolf pelts to become more wolflike, and used wolves' teeth as talismans to protect themselves from harm.

How dream analysts interpret it The presence of a wolf in a dream connects the dreamer to his or her wild side, which longs to be rid of our conditioning culture. The wolf is also tough. It can survive in a harsh environment by eating weak or sick animals, or in its role as a dream symbol, by devouring parts of the psyche that are no longer useful to us. The wolf is the aspect of ourselves that survives by any means. If someone you know appears in your dream as a wolf, interpret it as an alarm bell. At some level, you don't want to trust that person. Freud identified idealization as a defense mechanism, meaning that it often suits us to idealize the people in our lives. However, your unconscious mind can see beyond disguises. If it senses a wolf in sheep's clothing, it will present you with the wolf in your dreams.

Questions to ask yourself If you dream of a wolf, ask yourself:
1. Who is the wolf in my waking life?
2. What is this wolf trying to take from me?
3. How can I prevent the wolf from doing this?

Symbolizes the wild side of our nature, exceptional mothering abilities, the transport of the soul to the underworld

The Eagle

This most regal of dream images is also one of the most positive. Very little is written about the negative attributes of the eagle. Unfortunately, dream researchers have found that eagle dreams occur only rarely, so you may want to put it on your list to incubate (see pages 30–31). The eagle, because it flies to such great heights, is symbolic of expanding consciousness, or great power and influence. In North American aboriginal culture, it depicts the Great Spirit, or the creator of all things. In recognition of its strength, shamans often use eagle feathers to enhance their own powers and to heal the sick. Probably the best eagle dream of all is one in which you are given a feather as a gift. This symbolizes that all the attributes of the eagle are yours. A hero may also wear an eagle's feather, as his prize for exceptional feats of courage and valor.

How dream analysts interpret it If you are lucky enough to dream of an eagle, treasure the experience and consider it carefully. The eagle is the part of ourselves that sees the big picture. This macro-thinker is the source of our original thoughts and fresh ideas. If the eagle archetype appears to you, it may be because you need to take a new view of your life. Could you approach a difficult situation another way? Jung also believed that, in the realm of the personal unconsciousness, the eagle can represent the dreamer's father. This would suggest that the dreamer holds his or her father in high regard, as someone who watches over the rest of the family. In either case, whether it relates to the personal unconscious or to the collective, as in the first example, Jung was clear that this is a very important dream.

Questions to ask yourself The eagle flies high and looks down to spot prey. It observes situations without becoming embroiled in them, and this allows it valuable perspective. To work with the eagle archetype, ask yourself the following:

1. Do I have an issue to which I am too close to see the solution?
2. Where in life do I need to take an overview?

Symbolizes expanding consciousness, the father, the animal equivalent of the observer

How can I work with an eagle dream?

In Gestalt therapy (see pages 18–19), every aspect of the dream is treated as part of the dreamer. To work with the dream from a Gestalt perspective, you could explore what it is like to be an eagle, aloof from everything you survey. What happens when you see someone or something you like? Do you swoop down, take what you need, and then fly away?

The Owl

The owl is a mysterious creature. As an archetype, it harks back to the powers we lost on the way to becoming civilized. So the owl in a dream may be telling you to connect with that part of you that is close to the earth. An owl has excellent vision, noiseless flight, and can turn its head almost 360 degrees. An owl dream may suggest that the dreamer has the ability to see everything and be aware of danger coming from any corner of the psyche. Consider the context of your owl dream and your waking preoccupations. The owl is nocturnal, so it is associated with darkness and the moon. Darkness is the side of us that cannot see, and the moon is a feminine symbol. Are you ignoring the feminine side of your personality? The owl can help you acknowledge this part of yourself.

How can birds be messengers?

Jeremy Taylor, a Jungian dream worker, writes that birds in dreams are messengers of the gods, or symbols that bring information from the upper realms. We can, therefore, interpret birds in our dreams as holders of information about our higher selves. Does your dream owl bring a communication from the most developed and heavenly aspect of your self?

How dream analysts interpret it In Jungian psychology the owl is synonymous with wisdom. The wise owl archetype is familiar, especially if we read the stories of Pooh Bear as a child. In these classic tales, written by A. A. Milne (1882–1956), the owl gives Pooh the wisdom that he so clearly lacks. But Pooh, driven by his appetite for honey, often misunderstands Owl's teachings or ignores them. Consider your dream owl carefully so you don't make a similar mistake. The wisdom your dream owl shares with you will depend on the nature of your dream, and may be trivial or profound. The owl is sexless, and an absence of sexual desire is what helps to ensure the owl's objective wisdom.

Try this to gain insight Consider the list below and ask yourself what kind of owl you would be. Bear in mind that all owls indicate intelligence, in whatever form that takes.
  1. The barn owl—do you like to be close to home?
  2. The snowy owl—do you like to live in extreme conditions?
  3. The hooded owl—is it your habit to hide from things that are going on around you?
  4. The long-eared owl—do you wish you could hear everything that is being said about a certain topic at the moment?
  5. The burrowing owl—have you created, or do you need to create, a cave to hide in?

Symbolizes intelligence, feminine energy, alerts to danger

The Dolphin

A dream about dolphins is a rare and precious thing. Generally loved and adored, there is probably no other mammal that is held closer to our hearts. Why else would we want to swim alongside them and gain inspiration from doing so? The presence of dolphins in a dream symbolizes grace, freedom, joy, and serenity. It can indicate that the dreamer is lucky enough to have these qualities in his or her life, or is looking for them.

How dream analysts interpret it The importance of any archetype, including the dolphin, can wax and wane within a culture and through time. Dolphins were depicted as man's best friend in Roman mosaics, and they are much loved today. Your unconscious is, therefore, likely to view them positively. As such, a dream of a dolphin can be enjoyed for its own sake. You will probably experience wonderful emotions as you enjoy the qualities of the dolphin, its extraordinary communication skills, and the calming presence of water. If you are unsure why this symbol is occurring in your dreams, or what it represents, you can use active imagination techniques (see below) to open up a dialogue with your dolphin.

Try this to gain insight In order to connect with the dolphin in a dream, use the following active imagination technique:

1. Meditate on the symbol of the dolphin. Let your mind flow as freely as possible and do not direct your thinking.
2. After ten minutes, write down everything that has crossed your mind. In this information is the personal meaning of your dolphin and the message it has brought.
3. Ask yourself: If the dolphin was an emotion, which one would it be?

Symbolizes joy, serenity

Do dolphins dream?

The dream life of dolphins themselves is also worth mentioning. Scientists have discovered that they sleep with only one half of their brain at a time, so when a dolphin sleeps, one side of its brain remains wide awake. In this, as in many other things, they are truly unique. Even when dolphins are in REM sleep, part of them is alert and aware, whereas all other species are fully engaged in sleep and their dreams.

The Dreamer as Observer

In some dreams you may find yourself on the sidelines, watching events as they unfold. This suggests either that you feel no emotional engagement with the event your unconscious is processing, or that, as an observer, you are seeking to be objective. It is a great skill to see things as they are, and not how the dreamer would have them. Observation dreams may also be precursors to lucidity, whereby you are aware as a dreamer that you are dreaming (see pages 32–33). If you have several observer dreams in a row, you may be close to achieving a lucid dream. But if you have a sense of distance in your dream, your unconscious may be working to resist emotional involvement.

How dream analysts interpret it The observer represents the part of us that waits and watches for the right time to act. It is a mature aspect of the psyche. By not taking part in the dream activities or interacting with others, the observer stands alone. An observer dream can represent a traditional male approach to life, or it may show a need for a logical, more distant perspective.

In Freudian terms, not being fully engaged, being distant, or observing in a dream suggests that the dreamer is using the defense mechanism of disassociation. By standing apart and not engaging, you can protect your ego from pain or anxiety. However, disassociation has a negative effect when it builds up unprocessed energy or emotion. You may need to admit involvement in the dream scene and deal with the consequences.

Questions to ask yourself If you would like to work with your observer dreams to make them lucid, try the exercises in the section on lucidity. If you feel that your observer dream is telling you that you are distant from something or somebody, you can explore who or what this may be. Ask yourself:

1. What am I observing in this dream? What situation in my *current* life does this remind me of?
2. Which characters are involved? Do I know them? If so, how does this link to the situation in question 1? What were these characters doing? How are these actions relevant? How might they suggest a solution to the situation?

Symbolizes rationality, maturity, or disassociation

What is a defense mechanism?

Defense mechanisms protect the ego against situations that provoke anxiety. We use them unconsciously, but we can change our behavior if they are brought to our attention. Defense mechanisms are not always negative and can help to resolve our problems. For example, being in denial after we lose someone we love allows us to keep functioning. We have to feel loss at some point, but in the meantime we survive through the unconscious use of this defense mechanism.

The Dreamer as Controller

In these dreams the dreamer is in total charge. Classic examples include driving a car or steering a ship, or being the general in a war zone, the head of a tribe, or the president. On occasion the experience can verge on nightmarish. Most people are familiar with the panic that comes when control is challenged—when the car starts going too fast, or the ship starts to sink. However, these dreams can also be very positive. They can alert the dreamer to an area of life where he or she feels overly responsible. Or they may warn us that we have, or are perceived to have, too much influence over a situation.

How dream analysts interpret it In many ways the notion that we are in control is an illusion. If you believe that you are in control of your destiny and, in some cases, other people's, Jung would say you have a god complex. The dreamer as controller can be a manifestation of this. A mature adult realizes that although he or she has an element of control, there are always extraneous variables that can turn a stable situation into chaos.

These dreams can also be reassuring. You may, for example, have a dream in which you have to organize a complex set of computer files. You may lack confidence with computers in waking life, but in your dream you complete the task efficiently and wake with a sense of satisfaction. The computer is a metaphor for the mind. A dream like this shows that you have sorted through a series of thoughts, issues, and emotions that you were struggling with in waking life and reached resolution.

Try this to gain insight Are you too controlling? The following exercise is designed to help you begin to let go.
1. Take the dream report as recorded in your journal and underline what you control.
2. How does this relate to a waking-life situation?
3. Write down your fears about what would happen if you let go of this control. How bad would it be?
4. Consider the aspects of the situation you can control. Now identify the aspects that you cannot and shouldn't attempt to control. Try to relax with the idea of unpredictability.

Symbolizes confidence, the god complex, the superego, mastery

How do dreams work as rehearsals?

The dream researchers Antti Revonsuo and Katja Valli suggested in 2000 that we have unpleasant dreams as a way of rehearsing potentially threatening situations. Recent U.K. research showed that positive dreams can allow the dreamer to rehearse being in charge. In them the dreamer is more likely to initiate aggressive interactions than become a victim of them. The dreamer gains control, which makes it a positive experience. The dreamer can then carry that positive attitude into waking life.

The Dreamer Is Younger

Youth is a time when everything is fresh and you are free of responsibility. It is also a time of learning and development. Dreams of being younger often highlight an unresolved issue or developing situation. They can also suggest a yearning for a previous time when the dreamer was younger. In many cases these dreams also include relatives who have died, particularly grandparents. The context of the dream is important. For example, if you dream of a younger version of yourself at your current workplace, it may be because you feel less able than your coworkers. A grandparent appearing in that same workplace, with suggestions to give you about improving the situation, would represent the mature part of your psyche.

How dream analysts interpret it If, as Jung believed, dreams are compensatory, then being younger in a dream may suggest that you need to lighten up. Go have some fun like you did in the old days! On the other hand, the appearance in a dream of an adolescent can suggest that there is some kind of storm ahead in your life because adolescence is a period of our lives that we associate with emotional upheaval.

Freud would say this dream is a sign of regression. When somebody regresses, they use the behavior appropriate at a previous age to get results in the present. An example of this would be an adult resorting to a temper tantrum better suited to a two-year-old or a baby. This type of dream, therefore, would indicate the dreamer is anxious about taking on the responsibilities of adulthood.

Working with the dream If you dream that you are younger, it may be because an aspect of your self needs help. If you were a small child in your dream, for example, you may need comfort. Keep life simple: Eat well, sleep well, and be kind to yourself if you are upset. If you were a teenager in your dream, do something positive that you would like to have done, or wish you had done, at that age.

Symbolizes wish fulfillment, regression, feeling immature or inadequate

Is there something on your mind?

It is important to identify what age you are in a dream of being younger, and what was happening in your waking life when you were that age. Ask yourself, too, why it is that you are having this dream now. What has set off this train of thought? What light can your younger self cast on your current situation?

Finding Something You Didn't Know You Had

When you find something in a dream that you didn't know you had, a newfound facet of your personality is being assimilated into your existing one. Manifestations of this dream can include anything from discovering a room (or rooms) in your house, to playing a musical instrument that you cannot play when awake. Dreams of this nature can induce a mild sense of confusion and often leave the dreamer wondering where they came from. These dreams are usually described as transcendental, which means that they take one out of the ego state and into one where it is possible to connect with the universe. Sometimes the discoveries that are made transcendentally can result in major life changes.

How dream analysts interpret it In Jungian terms finding a new room, going into the basement, or catching sight of an unknown environment are all expeditions into the psyche. Discovering something in a dream, whatever it is, is taking the dreamer one step farther on the journey toward being whole.

Or your dream may be more down to earth. In one real-life example, a woman had a life-changing dream in which she visited a store. The store was full of interesting things, but they were all too expensive. She left the store, only to find to her delight that the owner had put a gift into her pocket. Through active imagination techniques, the dreamer later realized that she wanted to start her own business (the store). The store owner in the dream (the Old Woman, see page 45) had given her the gift of confidence.

Try this to gain insight A dream like this is a gift. It will affirm, validate, and show you something that you didn't know about your future direction or the events of your past. The meaning of what you find may not be obvious, in which case you can work on the dream using the Jungian technique of active imagination. Play with the dream as much and as widely as possible. Ask yourself: Where do I have a sense of wonder in my life? Or, Where would I like to have this sense of wonder?

Symbolizes creativity, deepening conscious understanding, and transcendence

Do you have a special gift?

U.S. researcher Kelly Bulkeley conducted a study in 2006 in which he categorized good fortune in dreams. A dream in which you find something you didn't know you had falls into the "finding magical objects" category. Whatever you find in your dream may represent an extraordinary ability that has been hidden.

The Dreamer Is Someone Else

Dreaming that you are someone or something else can offer you insights. Because all sense of your usual self is absent, it can also be a disorientating experience. You may wake up, for example, surprised that you are no longer a dancer in a cabaret troupe. Whatever form your dream takes, it is important to ask yourself why you were another person. How can this person help you?

How dream analysts interpret it Dream analysts have put forward fascinating theories in this area, relating to ancient ideas of reincarnation and shamanism. Jung also linked this type of dream to shamanism. A shaman is a man or woman who journeys in an altered state of consciousness in order to bring back healing abilities. A more scientific interpretation, however, is that your dreaming mind has become confused. It may be that an alternate character has your identity superimposed on it simply because in the process of REM sleep, the neurons in our brains fire in a different pattern from when we are awake. For Jung, this kind of dream was magical. It relates to the dreamer finding his or her true form. Your changed appearance may, therefore, be a reflection of your true self, at your current stage of development. Alternatively, your dream may be the reemerging memory of a past life. Jung believed in reincarnation and the possibility of memories of previous lives breaking through in dreams.

Questions to ask yourself Dreams in which the dreamer is someone else can be extremely enlightening, because they can uncover aspects of ourselves that we have no conscious knowledge of. To work with this dream, ask yourself the following:
1. If this person was you, which aspects of him or her would be most helpful and which least helpful in your daily life?
2. What was your dream character doing?
3. How can you make this activity manifest in your own life?

Symbolizes journeying, seeing the truth, awakening of the soul

What is the purpose of the shaman?

In North American aboriginal culture, shamanism is a recognized religion. The shaman (healer) takes journeys to another state of reality with the help of trance-inducing music and, sometimes, hallucinogenic drugs extracted from local plants and roots. When the desired state is reached, the shaman is able to interact with powerful spirits and to diagnose or treat illness in the community, whether mental, spiritual, or physical.

The Dreamer Has Supernatural Powers

In a dream of this kind, you possess a talent that defies the laws of nature. The talent will be required by the situation and, in all probability, your ability will come as no surprise. You may, for example, dream that you can see through walls, that you can breathe underwater, or that you have come back from the dead. A dream such as this belongs to the realm of transpersonal dreaming, whereby we seek connectedness with the world and all its mysteries. It can be as powerful as you are in the dream.

How dream analysts interpret it Jung believed that in such a dream we make contact with our soul. When you dream you have supernatural powers, you access the magic kingdom of your psyche and make use of its incredible abilities.

Freud had no time for the supernatural. For him, this dream is an indication that the dreamer's ego is out of control, suggesting grandiosity and arrogance. The dreamer may not want to admit to these feelings in waking life, so they are hidden in the dream. Freud's advice was to forget the dream, or else to ignore it.

The Canadian researcher, Don Kuiken, includes a dream like this under the heading of "impactful" dreams, because it stays with the dreamer after he or she has woken. Research has also revealed appearances of the magician in this type of dream (see the animus, page 39), and the priestess (see the anima, page 38).

Try this to gain insight If you have a dream such as this, try the following exercise:

1. Record it in your journal. Now honor the dream by doing something in your waking life to show that you have heard its message.
2. Do something you consider to be spiritual—go for a walk in the country, or go to a place of worship. Be somewhere, or with someone, that puts you in touch with your sense of the supernatural even when you are awake.
3. In the years following the dream, you will find it useful to look back and see whether, in a metaphorical sense, your extraordinary ability played out in real life. Ask yourself if your dream is relevant to your current situation.

Symbolizes extraordinary experience, the soul, knowing our own power

Do you believe in the paranormal?

More than 30 percent of men and 28 percent of women believe that paranormal events, such as telepathy and precognition, are possible during or through dreams. So a surprising number—almost one-third of us—disagree with the scientific approach to dreams that dismisses any possibility of these events taking place.

Wearing New Clothes

Most of us enjoy new clothes, and this dream is normally very positive. It may indicate that you are ready to show an aspect of yourself that you haven't been bold enough to show so far. It may also suggest improved health. Whatever form it takes, the dream experience will brim with positive emotions such as self-belief, excitement, and happiness. Don't be surprised if your dream self makes a fashion statement. Many dreams containing references to new clothes feature clothes that stand out. You may be wearing vivid pink shoes, for example, or a flamboyant hat in a room full of hatless people. This suggests that you are finding your own style and not only in the fashion sense.

How dream analysts interpret it This dream is about identity and change. Your choice of new clothes will tell you something about the part of your persona that is adapting or developing. In cultural terms, clothing often reflects our social rank, so this type of dream can also tell us where in our lives we are feeling more positive and have the most positive self-image. A dream in which you wear a low-ranking soldier's uniform suggests you are receptive to taking orders, for example, whereas a general's garb suggests you are in charge.

The types of clothes may also be telling. For example, in Freudian symbolism, a purse represents the vagina. Freud would say that new clothes generally, especially uniforms, are an expression of the superego, the part of us that restores or maintains the rules. In this sense the clothes we wear in our dreams may disguise our more primitive selves. Clothing may also indicate a disagreement between mothers and daughters.

Try this to gain insight This type of dream may bring a message of physical healing, especially in times of ill health. If you are ill, or could do with a health boost, try incubating a dream (see pages 30–31) in which you change your clothing. During the incubation stage, choose one of these scenarios:
1. Change from old clothes to new ones to herald recovery.
2. Find jewelry, or accept it as a gift, to promote good fortune.
3. Buy new clothes or jewelry or both to change your self-image or to improve your physical health.

Symbolizes identity, autonomy, recovery from illness

How do clothes relate to sexual health?

We often find we are dressed provocatively in our dreams, especially in dreams of a sexual nature. Gayle Delaney, a dream therapist who writes extensively about sexual dreams, suggests that our sexual style is expressed by our chosen attire. In dreams of this kind it can be useful to note whether your clothing is overtly sexual or is somehow restrictive, suggesting repression. What you are wearing will tell you something new about the state of your sexual health.

Dreaming of New Machines

Have you ever dreamed of an amazing new invention that will change the world? Unfortunately, it is not so likely to seem amazing in the morning. Nonetheless, a dream like this can only mean good things. It may indicate that you have at last found the ideal solution to a problem that has seemed insurmountable. New cars, new planes, new computers, or anything along these lines suggests a moving forward of the mind. The mind as a computer is a commonly used metaphor. Look carefully at the insides of your new machine; it may reveal the inner workings of your mind.

How dream analysts interpret it New machines in dreams allow us to draw on one of the most beneficial of Jungian concepts—that dreams are prospective as well as retrospective. Not only can they comment on what has passed, but they can also inform us of potential or future possibilities. Your dream may be showing you the way ahead.

A new machine is a symbol of masculinity. It relates to the animus (see page 39), the logical, nonemotional side of us that is useful in certain situations. This dream can suggest the cool execution of an action or decision that will result in personal progress.

Dream researcher Patricia Garfield has suggested that new machines or inventions relate to the smooth working of the mind and its ability to process large amounts of information. Using a telephone or a computer successfully in a dream, for example, is a sign of good communication between aspects of the psyche. The inclusion of machines can also relate to problem-solving activity. If you have struggled with your work during the day, a dream machine may give you that eureka moment.

Questions to ask yourself Ask yourself the following about the new machine in your dream:

1. What is its purpose?
2. Where in my life could I be more mechanical and less human?
3. What does my new machine do that I cannot?
4. How could I develop these skills or abilities?

Symbolizes new ideas, potential, opportunities for innovative development

How does new technology affect dreams?

As well as holding meaning about accessing new concepts, dreams of new machines or technology can also indicate movement from an emotional way of seeing life to one that is more robotic. When we learn new skills we have to concentrate hard to master them, so dreaming of new technology can signify a move to the automatic, the robotic—a shift from what was once a difficult task to one that becomes second nature.

The Dreamer Is Flying

Dream research shows that this is one of the most universal of dreams. Ask your friends and family, and you will find that most have had a flying dream at some point. The experience, which is normally extremely enjoyable, may be recalled in vivid detail even years after the event. The typical flying dream takes the dreamer high above a familiar environment and the people they know enabling him or her to look down in wonder. In some cases, the dreamer is ambitious enough to reach space and look down on the whole world. This experience is referred to by astronauts, who have admired the view in their waking lives as well as in their dreams, as "seeing the blue pearl." From such a perspective, the world appears both vulnerable and extremely precious.

How dream analysts interpret it By transcending the confines of the material world and our egos, we can reach the heights of development. This is not always easy, which is why learning to fly in a dream can be very difficult and you may hit a few obstacles. When we can finally fly, we soar psychologically and find peace. This dream occurs when you have worked out what you want from life and how you want to live.

Freud believed that all girls really want to be boys and that a woman's dream of flying was yet more proof of this. If a man dreamed that he was flying, Freud suspected that this was a manifestation of pride or a need to show off. The simplest Freudian interpretation, however, is that flying symbolizes an erection in men and sexual arousal in women.

Am I flying high?

Dream researcher Patricia Garfield suggests that, in order to understand the significance of our flying dreams, we should work with the metaphors listed below. What do the following statements mean to you?

- I'm on the rise.
- I'm in seventh heaven.
- I have high hopes.
- I'm at the top of my trade.

Try this to gain insight A dream of flying may hint that the dreamer needs to look at a situation from above. Psychologists call this a top-down approach to problem solving, as opposed to a bottom-up approach whereby you try to find the solution within the issue. You can try the top-down approach by meditating on the blue pearl as follows:

1. Use the image of the world in space to meditate for ten minutes. Think of nothing else.
2. When your mind starts to wander, bring it back to the image of a blue pearl.
3. Write down your thoughts and feelings.

Symbolizes being free, self-actualization, rising above

The Dreamer
Looks Fantastic

Dreams are often referred to as mirrors, and in this case the mirror is flattering. Suddenly, your dream self realizes that you look fantastic, perhaps slimmer, younger, or fitter. You may have a full head of hair and the muscles of Adonis. The atmosphere in this dream is of invigoration, rejuvenation, and health. Often, the dream boosts the dreamer's morale and brings a sense of confidence that he or she takes into waking life. We can all benefit from this kind of dream. Unfortunately, research has found that it occurs naturally only rarely, but you can use incubation techniques (see below) to increase your chances.

How dream analysts interpret it You don't have to look far for a tale that symbolizes the quest for eternal youth, and the looks that go with it. This dream reflects our desire to be young and beautiful. The moral of these stories is that what counts is inside, but our unconscious may think otherwise. Do you have sex on your mind? A dream in which you look as attractive as your imagination allows may indicate that you are on the prowl.

Most of us have wished we were more desirable at one time or another. The better we look, the more people will want us, and the greater the likelihood that we will find a lover or partner. Patricia Garfield classifies these dreams as universal. She says that this is one of the most positive dreams, indicating that the dreamer is coming out of a period of feeling ugly or bad about himself. This dream makes this transition conscious.

Try this to gain insight Regardless of the dream's underlying message, your immune system will be given a boost by your sense of looking your best. Try the following incubation exercise:
1. Sit quietly for 15 minutes before you plan to go to bed.
2. Visualize, in detail, the areas of your body that you want to change or to look fantastic.
3. See yourself molding these parts carefully and lovingly, as if you were made of clay. Make them exactly as you want. Try to imagine how it would feel to do this.
4. Ask your unconscious mind to give you a dream containing these sculpted images.

Symbolizes idealized images of men and women, the persona

Does physical appearance affect my dreams?

It is increasingly common for women and men to undergo surgery in an effort to attain a physical ideal. We know that radical physical changes are commonly reflected in dreams. A study published in 2005 looked at the dreams of a group of women who had undergone mastectomies following breast cancer. The conclusion of the research was that in dreaming we can undergo an adaptation process that results in the acceptance of a new physical self.

Being at Home

The environment in which your dream takes place is important to the dream's meaning. As with any story, setting also plays a major role in establishing tone. A dream set in a shopping mall, for example, will have a different atmosphere from one that has a summery meadow as its backdrop. The most common of all dream environments, however, is the home. The house represents the self, so it makes sense for it to make a regular appearance. One of the best dreams is finding a room or space in a house that we had no idea existed. This suggests that we are ready to meet a part of ourselves that we hadn't been aware of previously.

How dream analysts interpret it For Jung, the house represents the dreamer's psychic structure. Each room, therefore, contains a different emotional atmosphere and meaning. If someone dreams of being up in the attic, it sugg_____ mostly in the head, perhaps also a tendency to fa_____ dream environment moves down to the basemen_____ terms, the dreamer is taking a journey into the u_____

What exactly is in the basement tells you if the_____ the collective or the personal unconscious. Arch_____ and symbols belong to the collective unconsciou_____ and things that you know relate your dream to_____ unconscious. Where exactly were you in the hou_____ carefully the personal meaning of your dream ro_____ will indicate what complex (see box) the dream is processing.

Questions to ask yourself What does the house in your dream say about you? Ask yourself the following:
1. Does this house represent how I see myself now?
2. Does any part of the house appear to be in need of repair?
3. Is this house distorted? If so, what does this mean?
4. Which rooms or part of the house are in perfect repair? Which aspects of me do they represent?

Symbolizes the self, unexplored aspects of personality, sometimes unresolved issues from the past

What is a complex?

A complex is a set of emotionally charged thoughts, feelings, or actions associated with an object or set of circumstances. If you burn yourself in the kitchen, you might develop a complex about kitchens being dangerous places. Even the word "kitchen" may reactivate the feelings (fear), physical reaction (pain), and negative thoughts of the original incident. Jung believed that the energy caused by complexes can be destructive or instructive. Because we all develop a unique set, they help to make each of us more distinct.

Nature & Beauty

Nature and beauty are often reported in dreams that are defined as transcendental. Transcendental dreams leave the dreamer with a feeling of having connected with the spiritual aspects of life. In a dream like this, you might stand in awe before a sunrise, walk beneath a waterfall, or take in the outstanding beauty of the Himalayan Mountains, which your mind has perfectly envisioned without you ever having visited them. People who experience transcendental dreams of nature often comment that the colors were the most vivid they had ever seen. Even if the dreamer does not claim a transcendental experience, dreams of nature and beauty are to be treasured. They can indicate renewal of energy, inspiration, or invigoration for a task that lies ahead.

How dream analysts interpret it The landscape in any Jungian dream represents the psyche in its totality. It is the whole world of the mind, not only the self (the home, see opposite page). A dream of lush, rolling countryside indicates a healthy, balanced psyche that will be a fertile environment for further growth. Ideally, this is the kind of environment we would all enjoy in our dreams. A stormy beach with rolling waves suggests a more tempestuous emotional life.

A dream of nature and beauty can suggest childhood or a period in your past, when everything was perfect, or so it seems to you now. The unnatural vividness of the colors may be due to the gloss of nostalgia, in which case the dreamer would benefit from taking a more honest look at the situation played out in this environment.

Try this to gain insight Read the dream featured in the box on the right as if it were your own. Now ask yourself:

1. How could this dream be connected to an area or person in my life?
2. What would the lightning indicate?
3. Which part of me needs the energy of lightning?

Symbolizes a healthy psyche, an idealized view of something or someone

An example of a transcendental dream

"I dreamed of clouds that came down to the earth. They filled the horizon. Then, suddenly, they dropped close to the ground. I watched amazed as lightning was formed in front of me. It was made in the clouds and traveled down to touch the earth. It was beautiful. The clouds looked like brown and gray balls of cotton. They were alive with movement and were almost like smoke. The lightning was blue and silver. I felt like I had witnessed a magical natural event."

Familiar Settings

A familiar setting is one that is instantly recognizable and well known to the dreamer. It will evoke feelings of comfort and stability. Don't assume, however, that a familiar setting in a dream is one you actually know in waking life. You may recognize a setting in your dream that is, in fact, a creation of your unconscious. Dream reports of this kind are usually prefaced with, "I'm not sure where I was, but it felt familiar." The familiar setting in these cases is an area of your unconscious mind that you have gotten to know in previous dreams, which your conscious mind does not remember. We forget many more dreams than we remember, and visit many places that only our dream self has gotten to know well.

How dream analysts interpret it A familiar setting, where we move around without thought, is very often the setting we choose in order to work through our current daily concerns. Our dream self is free in this environment to work through whatever psychological issues have been occupying us during the day. Jung called these little dreams, because they reflect only the dreamer's personal unconscious.

In Freudian analysis a sense of familiarity often relates to a past experience. A known environment may, therefore, point to regression. A man in his early twenties may dream that he is back at school alongside his friends, for example. This would show that he is still dealing with issues from that time. A strict teacher in this setting would represent the dreamer's superego, the part of him that knows how he should behave, but can't.

Try this to gain insight If you are able to dream lucidly (see page 32–33), explore your familiar setting. Despite its familiarity, it may contain hidden objects, people, or extra elements, such as rooms, that will add to your understanding of the dream. Try to look at everything with fresh eyes and don't take anything in the environment for granted. What do you discover?

Symbolizes that which we take for granted, a previous stage of development, what we already know

What are familiar settings in dreams?

Familiar settings may include the house you live in, the area or streets around the place where you live, the home of a relative, or a place you have visited. The list is endless. Determining the meaning of this dream will depend upon your associations with the setting.

Bodies of Calm Water

There are many ways that water can feature in a dream. It may be a contained element, such as a swimming pool, or a large, uncontained body, such as a calm sea or a gently flowing river. In some dreams, water can also have the polished, glassy appearance of a mirror. In this case the water has exceeded its natural abilities and become magical. The dreamer can interact with water in a dream in a multitude of ways, but swimming or bathing is especially significant because it can be interpreted as spiritual or psychological cleansing.

How dream analysts interpret it Jung believed that large, still bodies of water are symbolic of the unconscious aspect of a person. His more personal interpretation was that water represents emotion. A dream of calm water indicates that you are experiencing a period of quiet, or that you are emotionally well balanced. The dream analyst Roderick Peters advises us to make a careful assessment of the volume of water, because this can tell us how much access we have to our unconscious, or how in touch with ourselves we are. A dream in which you are thirsty suggests that you would like to find out more about yourself.

Questions to ask yourself Have you dreamed of taking a bath? A bath dream can indicate a desire for renewal, or a metaphorical need to be clean. A scene in a bathroom may also symbolize the release of personal baggage or of extremely private thoughts and feelings. To explore your version of this dream, ask yourself the following:

1. Which room did you take your bath in? The place will be significant. If you were in your regular bathroom, however, you may simply be processing events of the day.
2. Were you alone in the bath in a strange setting? This suggests you are immersed in emotions that you do not yet understand.
3. Did your bath take place in public? This is a classic dream, indicating a loss of your sense of self. Take the time to explore what caused this dream.

Symbolizes birth, emotions, the unconscious mind

How common is it to dream of water?

Calvin Hall and Robert Van de Castle, in their 1966 study exploring norms of dream content, counted the number of times people reported water in a thousand dream reports. In 62 reports, bodies of water were mentioned, making it one of the most referred to "objects" in the study. They also found that women reported water more often than men.

Forests

A forest is a wonderful dream symbol, and one of the most mysterious. Forests are verdant, fertile areas, where towering trees support and nourish many different species. When the hero or heroine of a fairy tale enters a forest, we know that something monumental is going to happen, and this is just as true in our dreams. If the dream is accompanied by pleasant emotions, there are almost certainly psychological defense mechanisms at work. This is not a bad thing. It means that your mind has recognized that you are not yet ready to deal with a problem or situation, so it is protecting you from potential distress.

How dream analysts interpret it Jung considered a dream of a forest to be one of the most powerful dreams we can have. Because people across cultures and times have always dreamed of forests, Jung considered this dream symbol to be part of the collective unconscious. Along with bodies of water, circular shapes (the mandala), and other defined areas, such as houses, the forest represents the dreamer's psyche. The characters in your forest will most likely be archetypes or animals. Did you meet a unicorn in the forest, for example, or an animal deity? Use the guide to the archetypes (pages 38–57) to explore every detail of this important dream in as much depth as possible.

In Freudian psychology, you explore your dream forest as a means of exploring your sexuality. Much of the undergrowth is hidden, but the forest is lush and teeming with life. The appearance of the forest changes with the seasons, which can tell you where in your life trapped energy needs to be released. A wintry forest, for example, suggests a need to loosen up. Freud gives us a starting point with sexuality, but we may feel cold, or even frozen, in many areas of our lives.

What can the seasons symbolize?

- Spring—new life, new growth, new beginnings

- Summer—a period of calm, relaxation, warmth

- Fall—the harvest, the beginning of the end

- Winter—frozen emotions, the end of an era, a barren period of waiting

Try this to gain insight The following exercise will help you get the most out of a forest that appears in a dream:
1. Write down the dream in as much detail as possible, focusing on every aspect of what you saw and how you felt.
2. Write about any characters or animals you encountered.
3. When you have finished writing, dictate the dream into a recording and use it as a meditation.

Symbolizes protection, aging, the psyche

Pregnancy

Being pregnant is one of the most common dreams experienced by young women. Discovering that a girlfriend is pregnant, on the other hand, is a common nightmare among young men! However, being pregnant in a dream isn't necessarily related to giving birth to a child, and men have also reported this dream. Pregnancy in these cases can describe a state of emotional expectancy. This dream is good news. It may suggest a project in development or signal a change for the better.

How dream analysts interpret it Bearing in mind that every dream event, character, or landscape is part of the dreamer's psyche, a pregnancy can be thought of as the gestation of a new aspect of personality. In terms of development, it represents the stage at which we must nurture or care for the part of us that is growing. You may, for example, be encouraging your creative ability by taking a new class. In almost all cases, dreams of pregnancy suggest some kind of positive change.

Questions to ask yourself If someone is pregnant in your dream, ask yourself the following:
1. Who is pregnant? Even if it isn't you, the pregnant person may be an aspect of yourself. Alternatively, that person may have characteristics that you need or would like to develop.
2. How far advanced is the pregnancy? A pregnancy always refers to something in development; if not a literal baby, then a project, an issue, or a concern. What stage are you at? Is this situation in its early stages or almost at fruition?

Symbolizes new ideas or projects, new aspects of the personality, the desire for a child

Does pregnancy affect dreaming?

If you or someone close to you is having a baby, then expect your dream recall to increase. This is a symptom of the psychological adaptation you are undergoing in preparation for a major life event. Any dreams you have about pregnancy during this time are likely to express your unconscious anxiety regarding the imminent additional responsibility or your fears about being a parent.

The Appearance
of Family & Friends

Just as we do in our waking lives, in our dreams we want to spend time with those we love. In this sense dreams are a clear reflection of our waking concerns. The dream environment has an advantage over reality, however, which is that it can be adapted to make interactions possible. In our dreams we have the power to reunite with lost loves and enjoy magical moments in ideal surroundings. We can share everyday tasks with dead relatives and tell them all our news. These kinds of dreams inevitably leave us with good feelings when we wake, having renewed our connections with people that are important to us.

How dream analysts interpret it More than anyone else in our lives the people in our family can give us complexes (see page 68). For this reason, dreams about relatives can take a great deal of unraveling. The mind mixes together the images we have built up of our mother, father, brother, sister, etc. from personal experience, with archetypal, cultural ideas about these roles. Some of the information around the dream characters will be personal, and some will relate to expectations we have of them that we are not even aware of, which have their basis in the collective unconscious. You can help yourself immensely by taking the time to understand where these dreams come from.

On the other hand, the appearance of family or close friends in a dream may be the result of your mind processing the residue of the day. If you played tennis with your friend, your dreams may contain snapshots of the match. Family and friends feature in your dreams because they are in your everyday thoughts.

Questions to ask yourself When you dream of family and friends, ask yourself the following:
1. How do these family members or friends reflect my views of nonsexual relationships?
2. How do I perceive the family (or my friends) in terms of the society I live in?
3. If these family members or friends were archetypes, which would they be?

Symbolizes current concerns, connections to others, the personal unconscious

How often do we dream of families?

One consistent difference between men's and women's dreams is the frequency with which they dream of their families. Family members appear in 15 percent of women's and 9 percent of men's dreams. Friends and known characters feature in 31 percent of men's and 37 percent of women's dreams. If grandmothers appear, they are often in the kitchen of a family home. This reflects both the literal and metaphorical nourishment and nurturing that we believe our grandparents can give us.

Birth

Birth or new life in a dream is symbolic of a fresh start. This dream is often accompanied by positive feelings, including extreme happiness. The fresh start may be external—a move to a different country, for example—or may reflect a feeling that something is being born within the self. A dream of birth can also signify a new awakening or rejuvenated energy regarding a specific area of life, and as such, it helps the dreamer to find the physical strength necessary for this new stage. Sometimes, however, the meaning is closer to home. If the dreamer wants a child, this dream represents that wish.

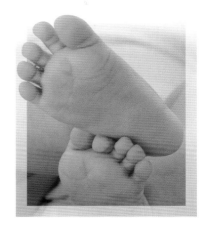

How dream analysts interpret it The birth of a child in a dream can remind us of what it is like to be a newborn baby. The complex (see page 68), or archetype, this dream would activate is linked to feelings of being new, vulnerable, and helpless. There is a newborn in us all when we begin fresh projects, new jobs, or do something we have never done before. At such times our internal mother needs to take care of the immature side of us, which is what this dream is telling us.

For Freud, nothing in a dream is as it seems. Every aspect is a condensed representation of a wish that needs to be fulfilled. So a dream of birth may appear positive, but when the event is explored in depth, it may be found to represent something else. The dreamer may unconsciously wish for the death of a baby sibling, for example, because he or she feels threatened by the introduction of a rival.

Questions to ask yourself To explore a birth dream, ask yourself the following:
1. Is the newborn a boy or a girl? Link the baby's sex to the anima (see page 38) or animus (see page 39).
2. What in your life feels like a labor at the moment?
3. How can you nurture the newborn in you?

Symbolizes vulnerability, helplessness, new beginnings

Does birth mean labor?

Giving birth in real life requires labor, but in dreams babies are often born with little effort. This suggests that there may be no need to feel newly born or that a task we are expecting to be long and difficult is, in fact, straightforward. You might dream of an easy birth from your mouth, for example, when preparing to give a speech. This indicates that you expect to enjoy the experience.

Entering Paradise or Heaven

Images of paradise signify perfection, spirituality, and in some cases, idealism. In this dream you come to a place where there is peace, joy, and beauty. Paradise appears in a dream to show us the psyche, or the true nature of our soul, before any of the trials and tribulations of life have occurred. In relation to this idea, it may symbolize the womb. Paradise or heaven is a place where we live without responsibility, but where all our needs are met. As well as our state before birth, it is also the place to which we try to return in our endeavors. Most of us want a peaceful, joyous existence, although the reality may fall short of the ideal.

How dream analysts interpret it An environment in a dream represents the global state of the psyche. Because most people's psyches cannot be compared to paradise, you may want to consider the Jungian principle of opposites if you have this dream. Jung believed that dreams compensate for what is lacking in waking life. Ask yourself the question: Is my life hellish at the moment? If so, your mind may have produced its own utopia to remind you that heaven is where we end, if we have done well, after all our striving.

We often describe being in love as "being in heaven." Paradise may show itself to you as a condensed image of romantic love. This may be positive, indicating that you aspire toward an ideal. Freud would say it suggested an unrealistic, rose-tinted view of the world or a wish to escape from life's difficulties.

Questions to ask yourself What does your dream of paradise mean? Ask yourself:

1. If paradise was a person, who would it be?
2. Is your view of this person realistic or idealistic?

Symbolizes love, perfection, idealism

A stranger in paradise?

The dream researcher Patricia Garfield, in her book *Universal Dreams,* suggests that dreaming of paradise or heaven is an extension of dreams of natural beauty. These dreams mean that some part of the dreamer feels transported to somewhere heavenly, perhaps because the dreamer is in love, or that part of the psyche has reached its maximum potential. These dreams may come to us as respite at times of crisis.

Getting Married

The symbolic meaning of marriage is union. Whether you are observing or participating in the event, this dream indicates partnership, commitment, or reconciliation. The marriage in your dream may relate to the coming together of two people, as it does in life, or it may represent an internal union of two different aspects of your personality.

How dream analysts interpret it Dreams of marriage can signify the union of the anima and animus. This union takes place at the end of what Jung called the second stage of development, when balance is found between the anima (see page 38) and animus (see page 39) in your psyche. This is the point you reach in life when you finally feel comfortable in your own skin. It's not a change you are aware of consciously, and it can happen at any age. You might have a streak of rebellion, for example. Before union is reached, your rebellious side may manifest itself as a bride refusing to say "I do." When your rebellious side is brought into line, your bride will allow herself to marry, and your instinct to rebel can be used positively, as independence of spirit.

Questions to ask yourself Rita Dwyer is a past president of the International Association for the Study of Dreams and has researched wedding dreams extensively. She has formulated a categorization system solely for marriage dreams. Which of the following four categories does your marriage dream come under?

1. The dreamer is the bride/bridegroom. This indicates that the dreamer is ready for some form of commitment.
2. The dreamer likes getting married so much they do it again and again. This suggests that your personality is fractured and out of balance.
3. The dreamer is reluctant to take his or her marriage vows. This can indicate that the dreamer is realizing the awesome meaning of commitment and isn't sure whether he or she is ready for it.
4. The dreamer is always the bridesmaid, never the bride. This suggests that the dreamer is not ready for commitment.

Symbolizes union, transition from one stage of development to another, being ready for commitment

What is the union of the self?

Achieving balance between the anima and animus means different things to different people. A wedding dream may mean that the dreamer is finally comfortable with being both intellectual and emotional, for example. All of us have these qualities in our personalities to a greater or lesser extent, and they will have been encouraged or repressed according to our life experiences. When someone is happy to claim traits of both the anima and animus in equal measure, he or she is ready for a dream wedding.

Parapsychological Possibilities

On an anecdotal basis, dreamers describe various types of extrasensory perception (ESP), including necromancy (magic; divination), telepathy (communication by extrasensory means), astral projection (separating the spirit from the physical body), and precognition. Precognition, whereby the dreamer comes to know something before it is confirmed, is probably the most common. You may know someone, for example, who has woken suddenly from sleep with the sure sense that a family member has died and who has later had this "knowledge" confirmed.

How dream analysts interpret it Many psychologists believe that paranormal experiences occur while we dream and that the dream state is more conducive to having them. The ability to have such experiences may be latent during waking hours but unleashed while we sleep. Jung believed that parapsychological dreams are possible, especially dreams of precognition. Even Freud accepted that telepathy may occasionally be enabled in the dream state, although he qualified this by saying that he had never experienced a dream like this himself.

Paranormal experiences may be seen to take our human capabilities to their limits. Because of this, people who claim to have parapsychological dreams are sometimes considered to be more highly developed. Other dream researchers dismiss all possibility of the paranormal, explaining such experiences as hallucinations brought on by the normal dreaming process.

Try this to gain insight To encourage your parapsychological abilities, start by practicing telepathy. You will need a friend.
1. Agree on a day to conduct the experiment. Ask your friend to choose an image from a magazine and to place it in an envelope. The image must not be discussed between you.
2. Before you sleep that night, incubate a dream (see pages 30–31) that asks for "vision."
3. After waking, write down what you dreamed about and place this report in another envelope.
4. Compare the image with your dream report. Decide with your friend whether you have hit or missed the image.

Symbolizes superhuman capabilities, paranormal insight

What is nocturnal ESP?

Experiments investigating ESP in dreams were undertaken at the Maimonides Medical Center in New York between 1962 and 1978. In this study Professor Stanley Krippner and Montague Ullman M.D. investigated telepathy and precognition, attempting to prove the existence of what they called Nocturnal ESP. They made some spectacular findings that other researchers have been unable to replicate, so the debate about whether ESP can be facilitated during dreaming remains open.

Prodromal Dreams

A special type of dream that is often ignored by researchers, and is, therefore, underresearched, is the prodromal dream. A prodromal dream is defined by Robert Van de Castle in his book Our Dreaming Mind *as "a dream where there is close correspondence between physical illness and dream content." In other words, the subtle or disturbed energies of your body communicate their changes and inform the mind that something is wrong by dropping hints in dreams. Prodromal dreams may indicate a physical illness that is about to surface, or is already present. They also indicate recovery or remission from illness.*

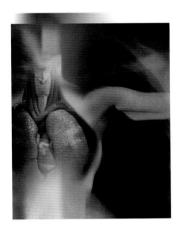

How dream analysts interpret it To be truly well, we all need to achieve balance mentally, physically, and spiritually. Dreams that contain prodromal warnings reveal a valuable internal communication process. If you wake with an uncanny sense that you have dreamed about illness, you should take the time to explore what it may mean. A prodromal dream can get you to the doctor in the early stages of a condition, before any symptoms appear. Several studies, including Wendy Pannier's work on breast cancer in 2005 while she was president of the International Association of the Study of Dreams, have found that dreams may act as precursors to a cancer diagnosis or to heart problems. The specific content of these dreams can give you a clue to which part of the body is affected.

Try this to gain insight A prodromal dream contains imagery that has some connection to a part of the body. A circular labyrinth may symbolize the anatomy of the breast. The images listed below can all indicate illness. If you dream of these or other symbols you suspect are prodromal, monitor their development carefully.
1. A damaged or broken car can indicate a need for work on the body or for repair.
2. A dying plant or flower suggests low energy levels.
3. A broken pipe may link to cardiovascular disease or illness.
4. Leaving behind old baggage in a dream may indicate that the dreamer is leaving behind a long-standing physical condition.

Symbolizes illness, remission from illness

What examples are there of prodromal dreams?

The researcher Patricia Garfield has written about prodromal dreams and reported on many real-life examples. She interviewed one man who dreamed he was traveling in an airplane when both the engines blew out. He subsequently developed a major chest infection. One woman dreamed that her dinner-party guests shot her in the heart. The woman saw the shots as acts of kindness because they allowed the pressure in her chest to escape. She was later diagnosed with a heart valve blockage.

Problem Solving

There is some convincing anecdotal evidence that dreaming sometimes gives us the solution to a problem. Every conceivable problem may be represented in a dream, and the solutions will be as wide ranging. The solution as it appears in the dream, in either literal or metaphorical form, is often experienced as an epiphany. The moment the dreamer awakes, he or she can at last see the way ahead. Most formal research in this area has centered on presenting people with a mathematical or logical problem and then letting them sleep on it.

How dream analysts interpret it To use dreaming as a problem-solving tool, you need to believe that the dreaming mind is equivalent to the waking mind in terms of its ability to provide solutions. The implicit conclusion of some studies is that the dreaming mind is inferior. One researcher, Professor Mark Blagrove of Swansea University in Wales, has argued that to solve a problem the mind has to pay conscious attention to it, and that this function is clearly disabled in the dreaming mind. The research of Professor Ernest Hartmann, on the other hand, suggests that dreaming allows for problem solving because certain associations are loosened in our dreaming mind, which may help activate solutions that were previously inaccessible.

Try this to gain insight Take the steps below to incubate a solution dream. For the process to work, the problem you are struggling with must be at the forefront of your mind.
1. Write down the problem; include as much detail as possible.
2. Highlight what makes you feel uncomfortable about it.
3. Write down solutions that you already know would resolve the problem.
4. Write down why you won't or can't act on these solutions.
5. As you prepare for sleep, repeat a summary of the problem, over and over again. Expect to have a dream that brings new solutions in the form of images, a story, or emotions.
6. Interpret your dreams using all the methods described in this book until you find your solution.

Symbolizes current issues, the need to resolve problems in waking life

Can dreams solve problems?

There are some famous examples of problem solving in dreams. One such story concerns Friedrich A. von Kekulé (1829–1896), a German chemistry professor who was attempting to describe the structure of the benzene molecule. Von Kekulé fell asleep in his chair and dreamed of atoms moving around in his visual field. Then he saw a snake with its tail in its mouth. He woke up knowing that the structure of benzene was hexagonal and that it twisted back on itself.

Pleasant Dreams

Pleasant dreams account for one in every three that we have, and differ widely according to what the dream is processing. A dream like this may involve spending time with friends and relatives, be so visually beautiful as to take your breath away, or be a great adventure in which you get to spend time with legendary or mythical figures.

How dream analysts interpret it A study of women's dreams carried out in 2008 by the Dream Research Group in the U.K. identified three types of pleasant dreams.

1. Dreaming of happy social events. These are dominated by friends and family and usually take place in a vacation setting or a familiar environment. They allow the dreamer to replicate and experience the connection we have with people who are part of our waking life even when absent.
2. Transcendental dreams. The second type of pleasant dream involves awe-inspiring natural beauty or magical events that would not be possible in real life, such as watching lightning being made or spending time with angels. The dreamer invariably wakes with a sense of wanting to make changes to his or her life for the better.
3. Dreaming of famous people. In the third type of dream, the dreamer is in social situations where he or she is interacting with well-known people, such as actors, sports icons, or historical characters. Usually, the dreamer awakes feeling excited and invigorated and will recall the dream vividly.

Positive dreams like these often express the dreamer's desire for contact with those they love or people they aspire to be like. Transcendental dreams often spur the dreamer to meet spiritual aspirations during waking.

Questions to ask yourself Look back through your dream journal and ask yourself the following:

1. Have I had a pleasant dream that isn't one of the three described above?
2. Which elements of the dream apply to my waking life?
3. What can I do to have more dreams of this nature?

Symbolizes psychological health, the desire to fulfill aspirations

Do pleasant dreams reflect a pleasant waking life?

We sometimes experience pleasant dreams in times of crisis. These dreams provide respite for the dreamer. For example, pleasant dreams may come to us while we grieve for someone who has died. It is common during this process to have dreams that allow us to spend time with the person we have lost and, as such, these dreams can be a great comfort.

Positive Emotions
in Pleasant Dreams

The range of emotions we experience when we have pleasant dreams is only just beginning to be understood, but some general observations are emerging. The most common positive emotions in men's pleasant dreams, for example, are excitement, happiness, and a kind of thrilled euphoria. In women's pleasant dreams, feelings of friendliness, love, and happiness are reported most frequently. Researchers have found that all positive dreams have their own distinct emotional themes. Some involve mostly feelings of excitement, for example, whereas others are predominantly ecstatic. These feelings also influence how we feel when we wake up. The Dream Research Group in the U.K. has confirmed that people who have positive dreams are left with a positive dream hangover in the morning that infuses their waking day with a sense of well-being.

What are transcendental emotions?

In a study of impactful dreams, Professor Don Kuiken, a Canadian researcher, made a distinction between what he called transcendental dreams and other pleasant dreams. The dreams he identified as transcendental stood out because of their content, which centered on success and magical events, but also because of the feelings they aroused in the dreamer. These dreams are known as transcendental because they stimulate feelings of awe, ecstasy, joy, and delight in the dreamer.

How dream analysts interpret it The majority of research on dreams attempts to extract what a dream means from its images, with the implication that dreams are above all visual events. Pierre Maquet, a biomedical expert at the Wellcome Department of Cognitive Neurology, London, and his French colleagues have challenged this approach with a study showing that the part of the brain that remains most active during REM sleep is the part responsible for processing emotional memory. It could be that the emotions activated during dreaming determine the images and other sensory information, including symbols and themes, that accompany them.

Try this to gain insight Which of the following assertions best reflects your experience of dreaming?
- If Jung's theory that dreams compensate for what we lack in waking life is correct, then unhappy people would have the happiest dreams.
- If Freud's theory that all dream content is disguised is correct, then the brain needs the capacity to distort or disguise emotions experienced in a dream.
- If Hall's theory that dreams are a continuation of our waking life is correct, then we could expect the emotions we have in our dreams to reflect the ones we feel when awake.

Symbolizes emotional well-being

Love

People often describe this dream in terms of the emotional landscape, rather than by reporting the images. A friend may tell you, for example, that she dreamed she was "in love." The experience can be very intense, just as love can be in our waking life. Almost all our dreams contain some drama regarding human relationships. Boyfriends, girlfriends, wives, and husbands appear with regularity in our dream lives. If you are concerned about these relationships during waking, the powerful feelings you have for these people will play out in your dreams.

How dream analysts interpret it Many types of dreams include love as a theme. This can be love for strangers or people we know that we are not attracted to. In this case the sex of the person we are attracted to usually means we need to work on the anima or animus (the opposite sexual characteristics). These dreams are rarely about love and usually about union. However, research shows that this type of love is relatively rare and that the most common types of love in our dreams are the love we feel for a sexual partner and the love we feel for family and friends. Why do we dream of love? It may be because feeling love in our dreams must have some benefit for the survival of the species. The benefit may be that these dreams allow us to feel connected to one another, and help to cement the relationships that support us in our daily lives. There may also be a physiological explanation for love in dreams. Feeling intense love in a dream is a good way of boosting endorphins.

Questions to ask yourself Your dream may be more about yourself than another person—this idea is supported by Jungian and Gestalt theories, which regard every component of a dream as an aspect of the dreamer. Ask yourself the following:

1. Who am I in love with in my dream?
2. Is this true in my waking life?
3. If the answer is no, which negative aspects of this person can I find in myself that I need to love and not dislike?
4. If the answer is yes, which positive aspects of this person apply to me, and how can I love these parts of myself in waking life?

Symbolizes security, reestablishment of personal connections

Can dreams inspire love?

In her book *Sexual Dreams*, Gayle Delaney reports that feelings of love in dreams can be more intense than ever possible during waking. She believes that these dreams, which women experience more than men, allow us to discover and accept aspects of our lives or ourselves that have been previously ignored. A dream of love may offer guidance and can inspire and enhance your current waking life.

Erotic Dreams

Sexual fantasies enjoy some airtime in our dreams. Men, in particular, tend to have dreams of sex with partners they do not know. Interestingly this basic sexual fantasy is often contained within the emotional landscape of love. A man may dream of meeting someone and falling instantly in love, for example, and this will result in them having sex. Women's sexual dreams are more likely to involve the woman watching her partner having sex with one of their friends, or the woman having sex with a man she knows as a platonic friend in waking life.

How dream analysts interpret it Sex features in surprisingly few dream reports. This could be because people are too embarrassed to share these dreams. The way people talk about sex, even dream sex, can be revealing. Sex in dreams can also tell researchers about society's view of sexual behavior as a whole.

Calvin Hall and Robert Van de Castle's content analysis system, which they developed in 1966, provides present-day researchers with a useful way of comparing sex in dreams for men and women. Studies using this model show that men dream more often of intercourse, whereas women report more kissing.

While some sexual dreams are clearly motivated by playing out sexual desire, some sexual dreams may be about something else entirely. Jung argued that dreams that appear to be sexual may actually be about unity. You might dream of sex if two aspects of your psyche are coming together. Freud didn't agree. In his opinion, people dream about sex as an attempt to fulfill a sexual wish, which they may be unaware of or prefer to ignore.

Why do we have erotic dreams?

Erotic dreams can leave us feeling unsettled on waking. However, dream sex often functions only as a symbol. A dream in which you have sex with your best friend, for example, may mean that you want to meld with those aspects of your friend that you have ignored in yourself. A same-sex sexual dream might tell you that your anima or animus (depending on your gender) needs to be reenergized. Dreaming of sex with a stranger may reflect a desire to unite with an unknown aspect of your self.

Questions to ask yourself To explore dreams of a sexual nature, ask yourself the following:
1. Who is having sex in this dream?
2. If these characters were aspects of you, which would they be?
3. What kind of sex was taking place? Was it, for example, gentle or aggressive, meaningful or meaningless?
4. How does this description apply to how you feel in waking life? Can it describe a "union" in terms of your relationship with yourself, in your work, or another part of your life?

Symbolizes cultural norms regarding sexual behavior, merging of components of the psyche

Friendliness

A dream that includes friendly behavior is often more complicated than it may seem at first. Careful analysis of the act of friendship and your role in it can give you valuable personal insight into how you relate to people in waking life. Are you forever offering the hand of friendship, for example, or are other dream characters always helping you? A dreamer who is often the initiator suggests an open sociable nature, and perhaps a need to have good deeds accepted in order to feel self-esteem. A dreamer who is always being helped suggests that an aspect of that dreamer's character needs some care and attention. The most balanced dreams contain acts of give and take, in which you are friendly with some characters and not with others.

How dream analysts interpret it Calvin Hall and Robert Van de Castle, and more recently G. W. Domhoff, used a classification system for friendliness, which will help you define your own dreams in this area. They identify seven types of friendly interaction as follows:

1. Offering to marry or commit to a long-term relationship.
2. Making physical gestures of friendly intention, such as hugging or kissing on the cheek (anything more is a sexual rather than friendly dream).
3. Inviting someone to a social event.
4. Helping or protecting in some way.
5. Giving gifts or a possession to someone.
6. Smiling or making other nonverbal signs of friendship.
7. Thinking friendly thoughts about another dream character.

Questions to ask yourself In friendly dreams, it's important to establish who was friendly with whom. Ask yourself:

1. Who initiated the friendly gesture?
2. What was the gesture?
3. How is this relevant to your waking life? For example, is there someone you need to make friends with or do you need to show yourself more friendliness?

Symbolizes how the dreamer interacts socially in waking life

What is the most common act of friendliness in dreams?

The most frequent act of friendliness reported in dreams is helping or protecting another dream character. This is followed by verbal acts of friendliness and giving gifts. The nature of these acts will vary, and there are marked cultural differences in what is an acceptable friendly interaction. For example, people in the United States give gifts in dreams more frequently than people in the U.K.

Experiencing Success

Achieving success is one of our greatest motivators. Many of us are striving to attain or achieve things that sometimes seem impossible in waking life. In dreams, however, we rehearse what it would be like to reach these goals. Although it can be deflating to wake up and realize your success has only been imagined, this dream can tell you how to proceed with a waking-life issue to get the result you want.

How dream analysts interpret it Sometimes success in a dream slips by unnoticed. It's worth reviewing your dreams carefully so that you don't miss any of your more subtle achievements. Good examples of quiet success in dreams are opening a door, managing to climb a wall, or being able to run although the dreamer's legs feel heavy. Just as in waking life, small steps, and the successful completion of each, are often forgotten in the bigger picture, yet each one makes a vital contribution to the completion of a larger task. Every dream success, however small, deserves acknowledgment.

At other times, our dream successes are magnificent. You may climb to the top of a mountain, for example, and stand at the summit, marveling at your achievement. Or the drama of the dream may center around some onerous task that feels too much to bear, then you suddenly break through this barrier and feel immediately relieved. Striving like this in dreams can be an indication of the dreamer's attitude toward waking life.

Questions to ask yourself If you dream of success and would like to achieve it in your waking life, ask yourself the following:
1. In which area of my life do I see an obstacle blocking my way?
2. What is stopping me from overcoming this obstacle? Is it a big block or a small one?
3. Did I overcome the obstacle in my dream? If so, how?
4. Do I need to take small steps toward success or make one huge effort?

Symbolizes striving for success in life, overcoming barriers

What would success look like in a dream?

"I was being held captive. I knew that if I could escape, I would be able to raise the alarm and save everyone. I also knew that if I tried and was caught, I would be killed. I inched my way to the window and spent the whole dream trying to pick the lock. Finally I managed to open it and jumped to safety..."

This dream report suggests that the dreamer has found a way to break free from someone or from a constricting situation. The life of the dreamer in the psychological sense depended on this escape.

Good Fortune

The defining characteristic of good fortune is that no one is responsible for it. It just happens and we feel grateful. Good fortune can be minor, such as the arrival of an anonymous gift, or it can reflect major psychological events, such as rebirth or a miraculous recovery from a life-threatening injury. Good fortune may also intervene in the form of objects. A locked door may suddenly open, for example, or you may jump from a window in a high-rise apartment and land on a soft bed of feathers. It is as if a dormant part either gives us an unexpected treat or rescues us from a terrible fate. Don't confuse good fortune with success. In dreams of success, the dreamer exerts some effort to make the event happen. In dreams of good fortune, it simply comes to us.

How dream analysts interpret it Good fortune can completely turn a dream around. Thanks to its arrival, a dream that was initially unpleasant can end with a feeling of relief. Good fortune is such a frequent component of our dreams and is so often unnoticed that dream researcher Dr. Kelly Bulkeley made a record of how instances of good fortune manifest themselves in dreams (see below). He noticed that these were often linked to the appearance of mythical characters and magical events. If an angel appears in a dream, for example, something miraculous may follow. Some analysts say these dreams can signpost the next stage in your life.

Questions to ask yourself Which type of good fortune have you experienced?
1. An ability to fly
2. Helpful sources in the dream environment, such as a car or train when you need one
3. The discovery of magical objects
4. The discovery of extraordinary powers
5. The ability to return from the dead

Try to establish whether the good fortune happens to other dream characters or only to you. This, and the context, will help you understand the purpose of your dream. Remember that neither you nor any other character should cause these events.

Symbolizes fate, positive experience

Is there a gender difference in the type of good fortune?

Research has shown that good fortune occurs in just under a third of men's dreams and in almost half of women's dreams. The two most frequently occurring types of good fortune are finding a magical object, such as a wand, and wishes coming true. All other types of good fortune, such as winning the lottery or standing before a vending machine as it delivers all its contents, are reported far less often.

"What is a television apparatus to man, who has only to shut his eyes to see the most inaccessible regions of the seen and the never seen, who has only to imagine in order to pierce through walls and cause all the planetary Baghdads of his dreams to rise from the dust?"

Salvador Dalí, artist

NIGHTMARES

Every night we dream, and in a lifetime, each of us will have more than 150,000 dreams. All dreams—even nightmares—contain positive messages, but how do you unlock these keys to self-discovery?

What does it mean if you have a nightmare about a vampire? Or that you find yourself naked in public? What do these visions reveal about the real events in your life? The trick is learning to decipher the symbolism so you can understand what your nightmares are telling you. Based on the latest scientific research, DREAMS & NIGHTMARES is an engaging revelation of the sleeping mind. The Nightmares half explores the nature and purpose of nightmares. With the help of interpretations from Freud, Jung, and present-day dream theorists, it investigates the generally accepted meanings of 50 nightmare symbols, conveniently grouped by theme. Demystify your nightmares and discover how to:

- Clarify what nightmares are and why you have them.
- Use your nightmares to gain insight into your life.
- Explore common nightmare symbols such as monsters, spiders, and snakes.
- Examine universal nightmare experiences such as falling, being a victim, and becoming sick.
- Keep a nightmare journal and discover patterns in your nightmares.
- Learn techniques for reducing nightmares.

This fascinating book will take you on a journey of discovery that is sure to absorb, entertain, and enlighten you.

ABOUT THE AUTHOR

Jennifer Parker, Ph.D., is a senior lecturer in research methods, consciousness studies, and addiction studies at the University of the West of England. Parker has researched dreams for 15 years and is a longstanding member of the International Association for the Study of Dreams and founder of the Dream Research Group at UWE.

DREAMS & NIGHTMARES

Discover What Your **Nightmares** Are Telling You

JENNIFER PARKER, PH.D.

Reader's Digest

The Reader's Digest Association, Inc.

Pleasantville, New York | Montreal | Sydney | Singapore | Mumbai

Contents

Nightmares

Why do our worries and fears loom much larger in the dead of night? We all know the stomach-clenching uneasiness that accompanies a bad dream. If you're lucky, you can shake off the unpleasant memory fairly quickly after waking. Unpleasant dreams, which may be disturbing enough to be called nightmares, vary in magnitude and effect. They may provoke only mild anxiety or be so vividly intense that the emotion in them forces you awake. A serious nightmare can leave you reeling and infuse your whole day with feelings of foreboding.

The key to reducing the power of nightmares is to understand them, and that is the aim of this half of the book. In the following pages we take a close look at the characters, animals, places, and events in our dreams that we recognize as nightmarish. Mirroring the format of the Dreams section, classic nightmares and their components will be considered in turn, alongside practical, step-by-step exercises that will help you explore what the nightmare means to you personally.

What Is a Nightmare?

The word "nightmare" has its roots in Anglo-Saxon language, specifically "mare," referring to a demonic visitor in the night. During the Dark Ages, women who confessed to having dreams of this nature were burned at the stake for colluding with the devil. Later in the mid-nineteenth century, anyone who suffered regularly from waking nightmares, whereby sleep and its visions intrude on waking life, risked being thrown into a lunatic asylum. These days, nightmares are regarded more scientifically as a distinct dream experience. Specialist treatment is available for people who are unable to function normally in their waking lives because of their severity.

Nightmares versus sleep terrors

Nightmares are different from sleep or night terrors, when the dreamer acts out the fear he or she experiences while asleep. These terrors happen outside of REM sleep (see pages 6–7 of Dreams), so the muscles are not paralyzed. Sleep terror episodes can be alarming to watch, but the dreamer does not remember them on waking. Nightmares, on the other hand, are distressing both while they are happening and after waking. They can occur throughout the night, with the most unpleasant ones happening in the first or second REM periods. Sleep terrors occur in stage 4 sleep, which comes near the end of the sleep cycle and is much deeper than REM sleep.

Did you have a nightmare or just an unpleasant dream?

If you answer yes to the following three questions, you have had a nightmare.

1. Was the dream so unpleasantly intense that it woke you up, or dominated your thoughts on waking?

2. Did the negative feelings of the dream stay with you after waking?

3. Did you have the need to be near someone and get comfort?

Classifying nightmares

To make their research more accurate, sleep specialists use specific criteria to distinguish nightmares from merely unpleasant dreams.

- A nightmare usually involves a threat to life, security, or self-esteem. The sufferer wakes up with detailed recall.
- Most nightmares take place in the second half of a night's sleep.
- A nightmare wakes the dreamer with its emotional force.
- Feelings from the nightmare linger after waking, affecting the sufferer's mood, sometimes for the whole following day.
- The dream experience, or the sleep disturbance it causes, may lead to clinically significant distress or impairment of social, occupational, or other areas of the sufferer's waking life.

There is some discrepancy between the scientific definition of a nightmare and what dreamers consider to be nightmares. Sleep specialists in labs only record a nightmare when the dreamer is woken by an unpleasant dream. Outside the lab, however, people often say they've had a nightmare even if it didn't wake them.

The nature of a nightmare

People think of nightmares as those distressing dreams in which they are chased by a monster or strange male character—people often wake suddenly as they are about to die. On waking they experience rapid breathing, sweating, or other physical symptoms of fear, and have the urge to tell someone what has just happened.

Case Study

This dream is recounted by a woman in her twenties. It is from a 2007 study by the Dream Research Group in the U.K. comparing the dreams of contributors with their most significant dream ever (MSDE). Over 80 percent of the MSDEs were nightmares.

"This nightmare is really scary. The setting is not at all familiar. There are no people in the nightmare apart from me. I am stranded on a huge spiderweb in the middle of a black hole. It is very dark and there is no sound or anything. The nightmare is about being stuck there, then suddenly I fall out of the web and wake up. Everything in the nightmare is red or black. I can still feel the web around me after I have woken up."

This dream relates to the woman's sense of being trapped. The sticky area of her life was symbolized by the web. She hadn't appreciated the significance of the nightmare's end, when she falls. She had no control over this. She felt that the dream's message was that instead of accepting her lot, she should make conscious efforts to change it.

What Does a Typical Nightmare Contain?

When people are asked to remember the most significant dream they have ever had, two out of three report a nightmare. Up to 80 percent of dreams are reported as being unpleasant, a finding that has been noted several times in large-scale studies. Research suggests, then, that most of our dream experiences are unpleasant, and that nightmares are the most memorable.

What do dreamers experience?

Nightmares that are most frequently reported involve a chase or a threat to life, security, or self-esteem. These are known as traditional nightmares. People also have quirky nightmares, which seem bizarre when recalled, and do not appear to be related to any concern in the dreamer's waking life. By far the most distressing nightmares are those where the dreamer reports the death of a loved one or someone who is close to them. These are called nightmares of loss. Deaths in these types of nightmares are unlike deaths in traditional nightmares in that they are rarely caused by other people, but are usually the result of illness, accident, or an environmental catastrophe. The dreamer is left bereft and may wake up crying, unable to believe for a moment that the dream isn't real. People who have dreams like this often want to contact the person in the dream to check that he or she is alive and well. In fact, a dream like this is unlikely to refer to an actual event, past or future, but usually has a very different origin.

Traditional nightmares of threat to survival and of loss both simulate two of life's inevitabilities: that we will all die and that we can expect to lose someone that we love at some point in our lives. These nightmares, which we remember so vividly, may, therefore, prepare us emotionally for some of the stark facts of life. They are experienced universally, have been reported throughout history and suggest that survival—our own, in the case of traditional nightmares, and of the people closest to us, in nightmares of loss—is of paramount importance.

What types of nightmares are there?

The following types of nightmares have been identified in recent research in the U.K.:

- Nightmares that involve a chase or some kind of threat
- Nightmares involving the loss of someone close to the dreamer
- Strange, one-off nightmares that shock the dreamer with their oddness
- Situations where the dreamer can't move
- Situations involving apocalyptic events

Can stressful life events shape dreams?
Rosalind Cartwright, Professor Emeritus at the Rush University Medical Center in Chicago, conducted a significant study in 1986 exploring how dreams help us adapt to new life situations. The idea that the experience of dreaming, including having nightmares, allows us to adapt to new or stressful situations is important because it means that there is value in contemplating our dreams. Cartwright compared the dreams of women who were going through divorce proceedings and found that those women who became moderately depressed by this considerable life change had shorter dreams and less emotion in their dreams than those who did not. So those women who coped well had longer, more emotionally intense dreams than those who did not cope well. Cartwright concluded that our dreams change according to external life events and that people who dream more about stressful events adapt to them better, even if those dreams are unpleasant or nightmares.

The most distressing nightmares are those in which a loved one dies. Dreamers often wake believing that the events in the nightmare are real.

Case Study

When David reported his nightmare to a researcher, he commented that its strangeness made it almost amusing on retelling, although his experience of it was extremely unpleasant. David dreamed that he had whisks instead of feet. In the context of his dream, the whisks were the result of a highly advanced surgical technique, but they made him stand out in the crowd and he did not like this. He ended up being ridiculed by an old woman. David awoke from his nightmare feeling dazed and confused.

With the help of the researcher, David realized that the dream was about identity, specifically his fear of being different from everyone else. He also identified signs of psychological growth and took encouragement from this. The old woman could be seen to represent traditional ways of thinking and, although he found the experience painful, David was prepared to flout these old ways.

The Sexes & Nightmares

Research shows that there are distinct differences between the way in which men and women dream. Studies suggest that women have more nightmares than men and that the nightmares they have are more emotionally intense and distressing. It would be easy to conclude, then, that women have a harder time battling their unpleasant dreams. In the murky realm of nightmares, however, the truth is never so simple.

Men's & women's nightmares

What do men and women consider to be a nightmare? The Dream Research Group at the University of the West of England carried out a study in 2007 that asked exactly this. Taking the nightmare reports of a group of 84 women and 46 men, they analyzed the nature of the characters involved, the type of social interactions that took place, the activities, and the general themes. Their findings were not what they expected. Although the women reported more animals and more instances of aggression, in all other aspects the content of their nightmares was found to be the

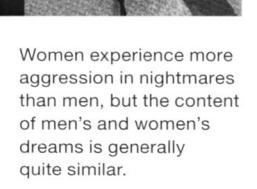

Women experience more aggression in nightmares than men, but the content of men's and women's dreams is generally quite similar.

The main threats in nightmares by gender

Threat	Men (%)	Women (%)
Survival	49	58
Security	46	52
Self-esteem	32	8
Integrity	32	16

Note that men are more concerned than women with threats to self-esteem and integrity, which are social problems rather than actual physical threats.

Source: The Dream Research Group, 2007.

Similarities between men's & women's nightmares

Nightmares that occur most often are at the top of the table. For both men and women, the majority of their nightmares concern the people who are closest to them. In most cases, too, their nightmares are about being victimized or losing something or someone precious.

Typical male nightmares

- Killing a male friend in a car accident
- Nightmares containing a threat or a chase
- Problem scenarios with women*
- Environmental catastrophe
- Strange or bizarre nightmares

Typical female nightmares

- Nightmares containing a threat or a chase
- Death of a partner
- Environmental catastrophe
- Strange or bizarre nightmares
- Unwanted pregnancy
- Supernatural nightmares. These might contain ghosts, incidences of precognition (see page 78 of Dreams), or interactions with dead relatives.

Source: The Dream Research Group, 2007.

same. Both men and women reported more family members and people they knew in their nightmares when compared to a typical dream. Both men and women were more often the victim of aggression or misfortune than in a typical dream, and, more often than not, instead of being helped by another dream character, the dreamer, whether male or female, was the one doing the helping.

So while women may have more intense nightmares than men, their nightmares are remarkably similar.

Psychologists have recently put forward the idea that men and women use sleep and dreaming to different ends. Women appear to carry their worries and concerns into dreaming and continue to process these issues as they sleep. Men report more pleasant dreams and researchers think this is because they use dreaming as an opportunity to play rather than to process worries.

When should I seek help?

Whether you are male or female, if nightmares are seriously impairing your quality of life, you should seek the help of a professional. In his book *Conquering Bad Dreams & Nightmares*, Barry Krakow advises people experiencing nightmares to visit a doctor if they recur over more than a six-month period or if they make you afraid to go to sleep.

Different Types of Nightmares

Nightmare frequency has been linked to particular personality characteristics, such as a tendency to be introverted or to worry more about stressful issues. It is also associated with creativity. Nightmares that are due to external life events, rather than the personality of the dreamer, can serve a useful function by alerting us to emotional concerns that we need to address.

Identifying types of nightmares

There are two different types of nightmares. The most common is the idiopathic nightmare. This type of nightmare doesn't need a cause, but just happens. The most frequently experienced idiopathic nightmare involves being chased or going through a life-threatening situation. If you have an idiopathic nightmare, you can work with it to understand why it is happening and stop it from happening again, to make your dream life more pleasant.

The other type of nightmare is the traumatic nightmare. It will be caused directly by an extreme event that has taken place in the dreamer's waking life, such as murder, violence, rape, or war. People who have been diagnosed with post traumatic stress disorder (PTSD) will often have traumatic nightmares that require special treatment. Initially, the traumatic nightmare will be an exact replay of the traumatic situation that took place. However, as it recurs over time, it will change and adapt. Although it will continue to contain many of the same key elements, there may be a distortion in terms of who is involved or the outcome. In all cases traumatic dreams are repetitive, highly emotionally charged, and extremely distressing. The dreamer may avoid going to sleep because he or she is afraid of repeating the experience. If you have this type of dream, you should not try to work through it by yourself.

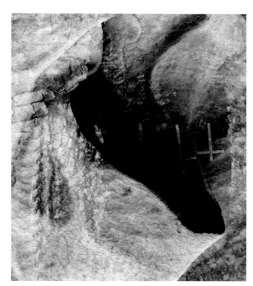

Distressing dreams fall into two categories—ones that don't have a cause and ones that are related to traumatic events that have occurred in the dreamer's life.

Idiopathic or traumatic?

The reported examples below demonstrate the difference between the two types of nightmares.

An idiopathic nightmare

"I was in the car with my cousin. The road was quite narrow. All of a sudden a car overtook us, just as another car was driving toward us. The two cars collided and hit hard. The car coming toward us was flattened on one side. I could see a lot of blood. I looked at my cousin and he was OK. We got out and tried to rescue the people in the car. In one car the driver was alive but badly hurt. In the back I could see a person on a stretcher, and I knew he was having a blood transfusion because there was a bag of blood with tubes coming out of him. We got them out and went to the other car to help the other people."

—MALE, 21 YEARS OF AGE

A traumatic nightmare

"We are in the car and I'm driving, just like when it happened. I can hear my friend, laughing in the back seat. Suddenly, out of nowhere, the car hits something. In slow motion I watch my friend fly past me and through the windshield. He lies bleeding on the hood, with his head smashed in two. I know he is dead. I can't move. I can't do anything, I wake up hysterical and trying to move so I can help."

—CAR CRASH SURVIVOR

What type of person most commonly has nightmares?

- The gender of a person who experiences nightmares is female.

- She is over 30.

- She has thin boundaries (see page 14).

- She is under stress or is anxious.

- As the number of adverse life events she encounters increases, so do the frequency of her nightmares.

The Relationship Between Waking Life & Nightmares

The frequency of our nightmares is determined by three factors. Researchers have called these trait, state, and environmental. Trait factors are the enduring personality characteristics that make us who we are. Are you generally optimistic or pessimistic, for example? Your answer comes under the heading of a trait. State factors are transient aspects of our moods that are unpleasant emotionally but not fixed. One example of a change in state would be the grief felt after the death of a loved one. An environmental factor may be a stimulus in the sleeping environment, which becomes incorporated into a nightmare, or an adverse life event over which we have no control, such as a tsunami or a hurricane.

Trait factors

Personality tests show that people who are most likely to experience nightmares have thin boundaries. This term was first developed by Professor Ernest Hartmann, former president of the International Association for the Study of Dreams, to describe people whose minds are sensitive both to external threats and also to their own unconscious fears and impulses. People with thin boundaries are more susceptible to external stresses and their own feelings. They also tend to remember more of their dreams than people with thick boundaries, who are less affected by events around them.

State factors

The pressures of life fluctuate, and the frequency with which we have nightmares reflects this. People with higher stress levels are more likely to have nightmares. Research indicates that women over 30 years of age are most likely to have nightmares. This would correspond with a time when they are likely to be juggling work, family, and relationships. Once both women and men reach about 60, the frequency of nightmares decreases.

Can a calming environment help?

Environmental incorporation can contribute to positive dreams as well as nightmares. Techniques are currently being developed using soundscapes, such as flowing water or dolphin calls. These soothing sounds are played during REM sleep to reduce the occurrence of nightmares.

Environmental factors

Have you ever fallen asleep and left the television on, only to be plagued a few hours later by voices calling you to wake up? You open your eyes to find that there's a movie playing on the television and you have incorporated it into your dream, which rapidly became a nightmare. Incorporation of this nature is extremely difficult to replicate in the laboratory, but anecdotal references to such experiences are common. Sleeping in a strange bed can also cause nightmares, simply because we don't sleep as soundly in an unfamiliar bed, which means we remember more dreams. As with most dreams that are unpleasant, we are more likely to remember a nightmare.

Adverse life events, such as serious illness, accident, separation or divorce, problems or concerns about work, or the death of a significant other, are also likely to affect the frequency of our nightmares. Unhappy events remembered from childhood, such as abuse (verbal, physical, or sexual) or serious illness, are also classed as environmental factors.

Unpleasant events that occur in waking life can act as a trigger for experiencing more frequent nightmares.

Events that increase nightmare frequency

These results below show how likely you are to have more nightmares as a result of a particular event or change of circumstance. The death of a partner, for example, increases your chances of having more nightmares by 16 percent.

Specific life event	Result (%)	Specific life event	Result (%)
Death of significant other	16	Family problems	5
Exams	9	Pregnancy	4
Argument or break up with partner	9	Adolescence	3
Changes in job or income	8	Arguments with friends	3
Moving	8	Bad mood the previous day	3
Chemotherapy or medication	8	Getting married	2
Depression	8	Other events	5
Tiredness	7		

Source: The Dream Research Group, 2007.

Nightmares as Warnings or Alarm Calls

Author and dream therapist Jeremy Taylor believes, "All dreams [come] in the service of health and wholeness." In fact, this is truer of nightmares than other dreams—a nightmare can be the most useful of all the dreams we have. They are undeniably powerful. People have described the feelings experienced during a nightmare, whether these are fear, sadness, confusion, or other emotions, as the most extreme they have ever experienced, asleep or awake. Undoubtedly, nightmares can act as psychological alarm calls. They shine an unflinching spotlight on what we would prefer to ignore and bring the problems that we urgently need to resolve to center stage.

Nightmares are often associated with underlying fears and may happen when we are facing major changes in our lives, such as leaving home for the first time.

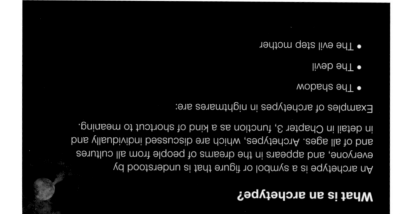

What is an archetype?

An archetype is a symbol or figure that is understood by everyone, and appears in the dreams of people from all cultures and of all ages. Archetypes, which are discussed individually and in detail in Chapter 3, function as a kind of shortcut to meaning.

Examples of archetypes in nightmares are:

- The shadow
- The devil
- The evil step mother

Reading the messages

Recurrent nightmares often become established when we don't listen to what our nightmares and dreams are trying to tell us. They may gradually become more unpleasant in order to attract our attention. The dream that is described in the case study below is a classic example of a recurrent nightmare. It was reported by a young man who had left home for the first time to go to college, and expresses his fears as he leaves behind one period of his life to start a brand new phase in his life.

The nightmare described in the case study stems from the personal worries of an individual. Another kind of nightmare, with its own particular set of alarm bells, may be what psychologists call "archetypal." Archetypal nightmares contain universal images (archetypes), and the types of nightmares link the dreamer to the concerns we all share as human beings, or to what Carl Jung called the collective unconscious. The warnings that we receive in our nightmares may, therefore, be related to our personal lives or, if the nightmare involves archetypes, to more general themes and issues that each of us has to face. These nightmares may be related to our spirituality or to existential concerns.

Case Study

"I remember my Mom and Dad are on an airplane. Then the airplane crashes, with my parents inside it, and I watch with a feeling of helplessness and sadness. I look up and see glass falling and an intense, bright fireball heading toward me. The visuals are very real, as is the sound of glass breaking, the crash, the aircraft engines, the fire, and the screams. I am so scared. I'm scared for my parents and scared for myself. Finally, I hear a voice that I don't recognize saying, 'They're dead.'"

—Arthur, college student

Arthur had had the same nightmare, or versions of it, repeatedly since leaving home for college.

When he related his nightmare to a therapist, she asked him to identify its three most outstanding features. Arthur identified his parents' death, his feelings of helplessness and fear, and the intense fireball coming toward him. The therapist then asked him to describe what message he thought the nightmare contained. Arthur's reply was: "Starting college is a new way of life that frightens me. Usually I would turn to my parents, but I'm on my own here, trying to be an adult." With this statement, Arthur acknowledged his fear of what was happening, and the psychological death of his parents, whom he had associated with safety. He didn't have the nightmare again.

Nightmares & Metaphors

Our nightmares often try to bring into our consciousness a truth, or truths, that we find unacceptable in raw form during waking hours. In a nightmare this difficult content appears disguised in the central image or symbol. When attempting to unravel the meaning of your dreams, whether they are pleasant or unpleasant, it is vital to acknowledge that things are not always as they seem.

One of the most extensive accounts of metaphors in dreams and nightmares was written by Ernest Hartmann (1934–), Professor of Psychiatry at Tufts University and the Director of the Sleep Disorders Clinic at Newton-Wellesley in Massachusetts. Hartmann explains that dreams and nightmares express emotion, and that the particular emotion being processed in the dream is always apparent in the central image or metaphor. None of this happens at random but is instead guided by the emotional concerns of the dreamer. This suggests that dreams are a type of private therapy.

Hartmann also describes the way in which the brain produces symbolic representations. To do this, he likens the mind to a computer, which is, of course, another metaphor. While we are awake, the networks in our brains, which are made up of millions of neurons, operate in a very focused way to ensure that we are fully functioning. During dreaming, however, these networks are more flexible, and this is what makes it possible for our brain to access more information and to make connections more broadly. Because this isn't a random process, our dreams more or less make sense. Their content is dictated by our emotions, which is why we dream about what is important to us. We may do this explicitly, or our brains may produce metaphors that can be understood after waking.

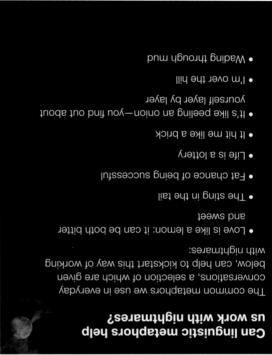

Can linguistic metaphors help us work with nightmares?

The common metaphors we use in everyday conversations, a selection of which are given below, can help to kickstart this way of working with nightmares:

- Love is like a lemon: it can be both bitter and sweet
- The sting in the tail
- Fat chance of being successful
- Life is a lottery
- It hit me like a brick
- It's like peeling an onion—you find out about yourself layer by layer
- I'm over the hill
- Wading through mud

Examples of Hartmann's contextualized images and the linked emotion

Emotion	Image
Fear or terror	Tidal waves, burning houses, gangs of evil men
Helplessness, vulnerability	Drowning children, wounded animals, being lost
Guilt	Loved ones dying in the dream; being unable to respond to those in trouble

Understanding the metaphor

A good example of a metaphor in a dream is a tidal wave. According to Professor Hartmann, this is a metaphor for being overwhelmed. To put it another way, a dreamer will visualize a tidal wave because he or she feels they are in metaphorical danger of drowning, or being engulfed. Other types of emotions that may be expressed in symbolic form in nightmares include helplessness, guilt, disgust, fear or terror, and vulnerability.

When trying to make the connection between your waking feelings, general ideas about nightmares, and your own unique take on the world, consider the ways the big emotions might be contextualized as images in your particular case. For one dreamer, terror may be most neatly encapsulated in a dream about wasps, but this symbol won't necessarily have the same connotation for another dreamer.

The concept of metaphors in nightmares is reminiscent of the ideas of Sigmund Freud (see pages 12–13 of Dreams), because it suggests that the real meaning of the nightmare is being hidden or changed in some way. This happens because we may not yet be ready to see the truth of what is concerning us, so we veil it in imagery to make it palatable. In dream work of any kind, unraveling the central image or symbol is invaluable in determining for the dreamer what the dream is actually about.

Dreaming of a tidal wave may be linked to fears of being overwhelmed by events in waking life.

Nightmare Interpretation: A Holistic Approach

Several explanations have been put forward as to why we have nightmares, but we still don't really know for sure. Although scientists and therapists may be getting closer to the answer, more work needs to be done to analyze the images, themes, and emotions in nightmares, and the ways in which they interrelate, in order to fully understand what causes these dramatic dreams.

The relevance of the nightmare experience to the dreamer

The explanations given for nightmares so far in this chapter concern only aspects of the experience rather than its entirety. We've seen that nightmares can act as warning signs, that they may contain emotions in the central image that we are not ready to face, and that other nightmares allow us to meet head on, with no threat to ourselves, the challenges that we all face as part of being alive and human. We know that nightmares, as a type of dream, are not uniform but are multifaceted and, therefore, may have multiple functions. One thing is certain, though: Any meaning must relate uniquely to the person having the nightmare, not to the therapist or researcher, who can only assist the dreamer in making the connections.

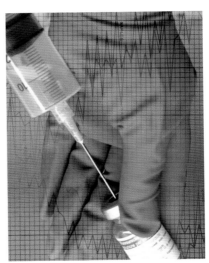

Taking medication or undergoing chemotherapy may increase the frequency of nightmares.

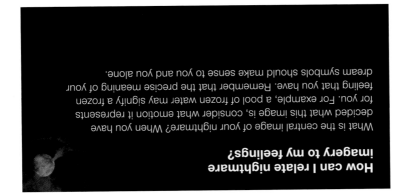

How can I relate nightmare imagery to my feelings?

What is the central image of your nightmare? When you have decided what this image is, consider what it represents for you. For example, a pool of frozen water may signify a frozen feeling that you have. Remember that the precise meaning of your dream symbols should make sense to you and you alone.

A holistic approach to the interpretation of nightmares enables us to benefit from, rather than dwell on the awfulness of, these experiences. Such a holistic approach takes into account all the factors relating to the dreamer: his or her sleep life, waking life, any medication that may be having an effect, and any issues the dreamer feels are important. The personal insights of the dreamer should be considered in parallel with all the professional theories and acknowledged in any practical methods used to interpret a nightmare and render it a positive experience. If you can use the experience of a nightmare to grow and develop positively, you are a strong person. A nightmare allows a dreamer to feel the emotions associated with an unpleasant real-life event or emotion and then accept what has happened and draw upon it to make changes.

Case Study

Brenda, a professional in her forties, had a recurring nightmare in which someone she knew and cared for deeply became distorted in some distressing way. Her boyfriend's face might start peeling off, for example. The nightmare began with her sensing something was not quite right, and with her being told by another dream character that she was imagining it. It always ended with Brenda being in no doubt that things were very wrong, while everyone else in the dream appeared not to notice. Brenda would wake from the dream confused and distressed.

Brenda's therapist encouraged her to think about what her nightmare was trying to tell her. To help her do this, they took a holistic approach, and talked about her life and past. Brenda was brought up by two alcoholic parents. Despite overwhelming evidence to the contrary, the problem was never acknowledged. Whenever she challenged her parents as a child about their drinking, they told her she was imagining it and that the problem was hers alone. She believed them, and had buried these memories. As an adult, Brenda's relationships had always involved subterfuge. She would accuse the men she was involved with of some misdemeanor or other, and then be told it was all her imagination.

The realizations Brenda arrived at while working with her nightmare were life-changing. It came to her suddenly: She knew the truth, and she didn't need anyone to confirm her reality. Afterward, Brenda was able to carry this valuable knowledge with her into every area of her life. She now makes different relationship choices and is happy. She has her nightmare to thank for this.

What prompted Brenda's realizations about her nightmare?
• Working with a theme and linking it to her waking experience.
• Working with the emotion and where she felt it in waking life.
• Finding the courage to face the truth and make any changes within her power.

Escaping Nightmares

There are three features of nightmares that make us remember rather than forget them: the ending, which is usually sudden and vivid; the detailed imagery that the nightmare contains; and the often overwhelming, unpleasant emotion that we experience. These three features are firmly in our minds when we wake up, and some people still remember them decades later. To add to our discomfort, nightmares rarely reach neat conclusions. There may be no proper ending to the story of your nightmare, and certainly never a happy one. This makes a distressing experience even more disorientating.

The function of nightmares

Our worst nightmares take place between 1:00 a.m. and 3:00 a.m., after the first or second sleep cycle. When you wake up, you naturally want to escape all of these bad feelings. You might turn on a light or make a soothing drink in order to settle your emotional state before attempting to go back to sleep. By waking you, however, a nightmare could still be seen to be doing its job. This is because when your sleep is broken violently, you are likely to feel a sense of urgency, which might help you deal with the underlying psychological conflict that caused the nightmare.

How many nightmares you have, and how often, will depend on what is going on in your world, and how these events affect you. Our dream life, whatever form it takes, is the most sensitive barometer of our psychological state. When we feel troubled or ill at ease, it will be reflected in our dream life first, before it becomes apparent in other ways. In this sense nightmares are mirrors of our stresses and emotional strains. They occur most prolifically when we desperately need the restorative benefits of a good night's

sleep—your brain won't let you have one. Unfortunately, waking-life stress and more nightmares result in a very tired person with superior recall of all his or her bad dreams. In these cases action needs to be taken to help that person return to peaceful sleep.

Freud (see pages 12–13 of Dreams) didn't think that we were supposed to remember any of our dreams, especially the unpleasant ones. He believed nightmares are spectacular failures because they don't do what dreams are supposed to do, which is satisfy our unconscious desires. Instead, nightmares reveal to us, often in the most horrific and dramatic ways, our unresolved psychological conflicts. They alert us through an extremely intense emotional experience to the fact that all is not well.

Antti Revonsuo: threat simulation theory

A more recent explanation than Freud's for why we have nightmares, and for why we remember them so clearly, comes from Antti Revonsuo, Professor of Cognitive Science at the University of Skövde in Sweden and also Director of the Centre for Cognitive Neuroscience at the University of Turku in Finland. He believes that nightmares prepare the dreamer to face threat or attack, by putting us through rehearsals of potentially life-threatening situations in a safe environment. His "threat simulation" theory is supported by the fact that, during dreams and nightmares, we are in a state of paralysis that prevents us from getting up and acting them out. Like a computer game, our mind simulates a challenging environment and allows us to stretch our experience by experiencing threatening scenarios. We might not ordinarily expect these events to happen in real life, but if the worst happens, our nightmares will have prepared us.

Can we see the positive in nightmares?

Nightmares often bring the instinctual into the rational. That is, they convert what we don't officially know into what we know. Keeping tabs on your bad dreams, and becoming familiar with them over time, will prove invaluable. As you begin to explore using the exercises in this book, you will notice that characters or events repeat themselves and begin to adapt and unfold. You will also observe how they are overcome as you deal with the problems that they represent, and how they are then reincorporated harmlessly into your psyche, or dream world.

Defusing the Aftermath of Nightmares

The intensity of the nightmare hangover is what makes nightmares so difficult to forget. When you wake up feeling either terrified or desperately sad, having mentally experienced a threat to your life or the death of someone you love, it may be impossible to view your day positively. Nightmare hangovers cannot be ignored and shouldn't be. To treat them effectively, it helps to look at the problem in two areas. The first is the acute distress that grips the nightmare dreamer immediately after he or she wakes. The other aspect of the hangover is the chronic or longer-term effects that develop over time if you have nightmares on a regular basis.

Acute effects

As well as feeling the effects psychologically and physically, some nightmare dreamers still see material from their nightmares after they've woken up. These intrusions may manifest themselves as blobs of color, misty swirls, or other visual disturbances. Or they may have the feeling that a character from their nightmare is still in the room. Like anyone who has had a nightmare, on waking these people will look for comfort, usually by turning on a light and consciously telling themselves that they are awake. This confirmation of reality, together with an acknowledgment of the hallucinatory nature of the nightmare, is a vital part of dispelling a nightmare's immediate aftereffects.

If you are very distressed by a nightmare, do something physical. You could get up and make a drink, for example, or turn on the television. If you have nightmares regularly, you might want to place a music player or radio next to the bed especially for this purpose. Doing something, whatever that may be, is recommended because it will help you become more awake. You may lose an hour's sleep, but it will help you put your nightmare behind you and reorientate your state of mind to one that is more conducive to uneventful sleep.

What is sleep paralysis?

Have you ever woken up and discovered that you cannot move? This is sleep paralysis, and it is almost always accompanied by a feeling of terror. In one out of three cases, sleep paralysis also involves a strong sense that there is someone or something else in the room. Occasionally, you will actually see a figure, shape, or animal at the end of the bed and might even feel its touch. In extreme cases, this presence seems like a personification of evil.

How to reframe your fear of nightmares

- Think about the last nightmare you had and what may have caused it.

- Ask yourself honestly: What are the benefits of being afraid of having this dream again?

- Instead of thinking of your nightmare as a negative experience, ask yourself what you can learn from it. Separate the nightmare from its aftereffects and look for its positive intention.

- Use reverse psychology by telling yourself that you want to have this nightmare, but this time you want to change it in some way.

- Ask yourself which part of you objects to losing your fear of the nightmare.

Chronic aftereffects of nightmares

The chronic aftereffects of nightmares can build up over time and lead to clinophobia, which is a waking dread of sleep. Although the nightmares themselves may not be real, the consequences of having them in these serious cases are tangible problems that erode our feeling of well-being in everyday life. Other long-term consequences may include restless sleep, sleepiness during the day, and increased anxiety. Many people who have nightmares may also become afraid of the dark to some extent, but at the same time they are often too embarrassed to talk about this new fear.

Any of these factors, together or alone, can impact upon sleep quality. As sleep serves to regulate mood, help memory recall and assist in growth in young people, and provides restorative qualities no matter what age we are, it is important that nightmares do not supersede a person's natural inclination to sleep. If nightmares are occurring more than once or twice a month and there is no external cause, such as trauma, nor any current significant life event, it may be wise to visit a doctor just to talk through efficient sleep hygiene.

The chronic effects of nightmares are best tackled with cognitive therapy, which will focus on reframing the fear that is at the heart of the problem. Even in less serious cases, changing the way you think about nightmares will radically alter how they affect you. Reframing them in this way (see box above) can eliminate the negative impact of nightmares in a surprisingly short period of time.

A crowd of menacing people may feature in traditional nightmares.

Keeping a Nightmare Journal

The idea of keeping a record of your nightmares may not fill you with instant enthusiasm. It means having to take the unpleasant feelings that were present in your nightmares into your waking life, and to some extent re-entering the experience. For many, however, this difficult process is the key to freedom. Sleep disorders specialist Barry Krakow, M.D., believes it is one of the most effective methods of eliminating nightmares completely.

Recording your nightmares

1. Write down your nightmare in the first person and present tense. Record as much detail as possible. Leave lines free so you can include more details if you remember them later.
2. Consider every aspect of the dream in your report, not only the visual imagery. What was the atmosphere like, for example? Did the nightmare have a particular energy?
3. Select the elements of the nightmare that stand out for you. These may be characters, for example, or images, or symbols. Underline them in the text.
4. What do you associate with these outstanding features? Write down whatever comes to mind.
5. Now explore the relationships between

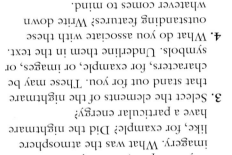

Images and symbols are part of a universal visual language that you do not need language to interpret.

If you were a movie, which would you be?

Jung believed that big dreams, or nightmares, tell the story of our lives and the roles we have cast ourselves. Just like in the movies, our dreams are based on universal themes and archetypal characters. In the story of life, as seen through the lens of a nightmare, women might find themselves captive, as a victim, or as a princess who has to marry a wicked prince. Men might imagine themselves as heroes desperately trying, but failing, to save the world or someone in distress. A nightmare will demonstrate the dreamer's psychological block, which keeps him or her from the happy ending we all feel we deserve.

An example of a nightmare report

"I am in the dark, I cannot see, I sense that someone or something is hiding in the shadows. I think I know it or them, but I can't be sure. It occurs to me that they are bringing something bad, I know the end is coming! I feel an increasing sense of panic."

(See pages 30–31 for a discussion of this nightmare.)

Reflecting & gaining perspective

1. Once you have written down your nightmare and worked with it, take time to reflect upon the process. Acknowledge that the nightmare no longer resides inside you but is manifested outside, in your written report. One useful way to gain perspective is to ask yourself what you would tell a friend who'd had your dream. What would you tell your friend that it meant?

2. As you become proficient at recording and understanding your nightmares, you will develop your own particular questions or focus on aspects of the dream that relate to your own experience. You will become your own expert.

3. After recording a nightmare, do something pleasant to take your mind off it.

yourself and all the other characters in the nightmare. Were the relationships equal? How exactly were they unequal? If these shady figures were part of your personality, which parts would they represent? If you dreamed of a hooded figure, for example, consider whether there is a part of yourself that you keep hidden. How might these attributes be associated with those people who are close to you in waking life?

6. Once you've worked with the questions in step five, ask yourself what connections exist between this nightmare and your current or past life. Is your nightmare related to any waking situation that has yet to be resolved?

7. Widen your thinking. Move beyond your own story and life to explore the links with other stories, myths, and what is happening in society and our culture in general.

What is a symbol?

Symbols exist as part of a universal language that everyone can understand regardless of personal circumstances or cultural background. One symbol can represent a thousand words of description. Consider a drawing of a sun, for example, and contrast it with a cloud. There's more to them than the weather! Symbols make meaning accessible to everyone, if they are brave enough to seek it.

Techniques for Reducing Nightmares

Any approach to dream or nightmare work should be tailored to the dreamer. What works for one person may not necessarily work for someone else, who may have a completely different view of the world. A nightmare dreamer may simply want the nightmares to stop and not be interested in drawing any psychological meaning or benefit from them. For these people, there are tried and tested methods that will make their nightmares go away without the need for self-examination.

Changing the way we think about nightmares

Central to this approach is the ongoing interactive relationship between waking life and nightmares. What comes first, your life or your nightmares? It's like the chicken-or-egg question, but the idea behind it is that if nightmares are not rehearsed, thought about, or given any emotional attention during your waking life, then they will not come to you when you go to sleep. Barry Krakow allows his patients to tell a nightmare just once, then urges them to stop rehearsing it or thinking about it. If the nightmare continues to be an emotional concern in waking life, it will continue to occur. Krakow's technique attempts to take the power out of the nightmare by reducing the attention the person having the nightmare pays to it.

Reducing nightmares requires active participation. A typical, and understandable, reaction to these nightly events is the ostrich approach, whereby we stick our heads in the sand and ignore them. If we want the nightmares to go away, we have to unlearn, or reconstruct, our thought processes to engage with the nightmare. There is an old Native American proverb that refers to the dark and light side of human natures: "There are two wild dogs fighting in us all; one is light, the other is dark. The one that you feed the most will win." This saying certainly applies to nightmare reduction. All remedies and techniques require active participation and patience.

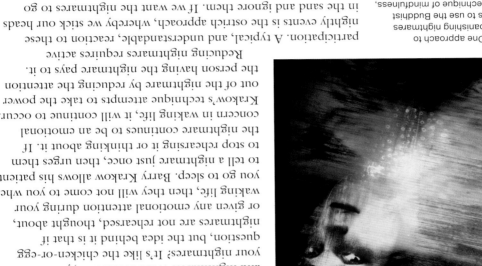

One approach to banishing nightmares is to use the Buddhist technique of mindfulness, or living in the moment.

Desensitization, distraction & extinction techniques

The techniques below have their basis in the complex relationship between our waking and dreaming mind, helping us to realize how they are inextricably linked. To use them, you will need patience and perseverance. Your nightmares will not stop immediately, but with continued endeavor they will either stop or at least become less severe.

1. Write down the nightmare on a piece of paper and then burn the paper. Let it go. It's done. From this moment on, make an active decision not to think about the nightmare again. This is known as desensitization. Desensitization allows you to externalize the nightmare by putting it down on paper and making it safe. Through the process of writing it down and facing your nightmare, you are also beginning what is called cognitive restructuring (see technique 2, below).

2. During your waking life, try to associate the word nightmare with something pleasant. It should be something that makes you smile or feel happy. "Puppy" is a good example. Every time the word nightmare or anything associated with nightmares crops up, think "puppy" and your mind will get into the habit of a pleasant response. This technique is called cognitive restructuring.

3. Use distraction when you prepare for sleep. Listen to either music or relaxation tapes that are calming and positive. This technique will distract you from the nightmare and prevent you from worrying about the possibility of having one.

4. Finally, you can put an end to nightmares by practicing mindfulness. This is a Buddhist principle that essentially means staying, or being, in the moment. Using this extinction technique keeps your mind focused on the real world you are living in. There is no past or future, just the moment. In the moment, there are no nightmares to fear, no issues to resolve, and no psychological distress to face—there is only the now. Practicing mindfulness will not only reduce nightmares, but being "in the now" makes you feel calm and safe, so it can also bring stress relief during the day.

Reducing nightmares using imagery rehearsal therapy

Once you have recorded your nightmare using the method described on pages 26–27, take the following steps:

1. Open your journal and read what you have written about your nightmare. Your report should be in the present tense. Re-enter the nightmare. Do whatever you can to make the nightmare as real as you can during waking.

2. Acknowledge how the content and experience of this nightmare are connected to you. Now, while you are immersed in the emotions that it causes, decide to take positive action to change its outcome.

3. Say out loud that you are now in control of this nightmare. Really feel that you are in control. Tell it to STOP.

4. Make friends with or become the parent of any of the symbols of images that the nightmare presents. This method works at an unconscious level and is probably the most effective of them all.

5. Decide what changes you want to make to the nightmare and to the life event it is linked to.

6. Rehearse these changes to the imagery over and over again during waking. This makes your decision conscious and will elicit a feeling of control generally.

7. Change the ending into something positive that works in your favor. Remember that whatever change you make, you can't hurt anyone. This is only a nightmare!

Imagery rehearsal therapy & dream reorganization techniques

By far the most successful and fastest way to reduce nightmares is by combining two techniques known as imagery rehearsal therapy and dream reorganization. Imagery rehearsal therapy involves changing specific parts of the dream into images that are no longer frightening. Dream reorganizations involve changing the story, particularly the ending, into one that is pleasant or empowering. These two techniques are very quick to work and are successful in reducing both idiopathic and traumatic nightmares (see pages 12–13).

You can follow the step-by-step instructions in the box above to try these techniques for yourself. Don't give up if the nightmare doesn't stop immediately. Most people see a reduction after four or five days. However, you may have to carry out the exercises several times and attempt different reorganizations. If you don't see an improvement within a few weeks, you may need help from a specialist. Research shows, however, that people who use these techniques are gradually able to make them an integrated part of their waking life, and their approach to it. This has the beneficial effect of decreasing anxiety overall and boosting confidence in your ability to solve your own problems.

How to reorganize a nightmare

The following nightmare was used on page 27 as an example of a recorded nightmare:

"I am in the dark. I cannot see. I sense that someone or something is hiding in the shadows. I think I know it or them, but I can't be sure. It occurs to me that they are bringing something bad. I know the end is coming! I feel an increasing sense of panic."

In this rewrite, the story of the nightmare has been reorganized in a way that puts the dreamer in control:

"I realize that the thing is hiding because it is scared of me! I put out my hand and I say, 'No matter how ugly you are or how horrible, I really want to meet you and hear what you have to tell me.' I invite it into the light, and it shrinks into a small, harmless creature. It says, 'I'm called nightmare, and this is the end for me.' I hold it and thank it for keeping the nightmare for me. I let it go, and we are both free."

Reorganizing the story in a nightmare can put the dreamer in control and banish further episodes.

Cognitive approach & cognitive style

Cognitive approaches are used extensively in psychology and therapy. Cognitive means "the process of thought." Individuals tend to have their own cognitive style. You might, for example, be a positive or negative thinker, or a divergent or lateral thinker. When trying to alter your nightmares with the cognitive approach, you will need to examine your particular cognitive style and schemas (see below) in order to make the necessary adjustments.

Cognitive schemas

These are the emotions, perceptions, images, and personal behaviors that relate to any given situation in waking life. Once activated, one of the components of the schema cannot be felt without the others. For example, a bear may arouse extreme fear. It has a visual image that can be linked quickly to aggression, and it is perceived as a danger because it can attack and kill. In a nightmare the bear schema may be activated, producing in your mind a huge, ferocious, almost fantastical wild creature that will have some visual similarity to a bear. The dreamer will naturally react in the schema by panicking and running away.

Lucid Nightmares

We describe a lucid dream as one in which we know that we are dreaming. When you have a dream like this, you have the mental capacity to say "this is a dream." A lucid nightmare is slightly more complicated. Although you know you are having a nightmare, you do not have the sense of being able to direct any of the imagery, as you do when you are having a lucid dream. The nightmare continues to self-generate while you look on and ends when you wake up, either because the imagery was so terrifying that it forced you awake or because in your lucid state you woke yourself up. So if you find you can change the story of your bad dream, it is not a true nightmare. What else would you expect? It's far more nightmarish for nasty things to happen while you remain helpless.

When you have a lucid nightmare, you are unable to control what happens.

How to make nightmares lucid

Working with nightmares lucidly, in order to change them, is not at all the same as experiencing a lucid nightmare, as defined above. It refers to an increasingly popular method of helping people to escape nightmares, particularly recurring ones, in which the person

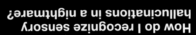

How do I recognize sensory hallucinations in a nightmare?

Many people experience what are known as hypnagogic hallucinations as they drift off to sleep. Common examples are:

- Someone calling your name.
- Seeing strange, distorted faces in front of your eyes where your eyelids should be.

More severe examples are:

- Feeling your body, or part of it, become strangely distorted.
- Smelling something strange.
- A feeling of falling, then stopping suddenly, which makes you feel wide awake again. This is the most commonly experienced hallucination of this type.

induces what psychologists call the lucid state. In the lucid state, you are aware that you are dreaming, or having a nightmare, and you make a concerted effort to change the story. The nightmare described in the case study below could, therefore, be worked with in the following way:

- I know that I am having a nightmare. The environment is awful and a demon is coming to get me.
- I am lucid. I know that I can change aspects of this dream.
- I decide to change the demon.
- I look directly at the demon.
- I change the demon into a fluffy pink rabbit with the most welcoming blue eyes.
- I use my imagination to make the web disappear so I can move.
- I walk toward the rabbit. I pick it up, and I stroke it.
- I affirm what a wonderful dream this has become.
- I know that I have conquered my demon and resolve to take this feeling into waking.

How can you induce lucidity?

It is not easy to train yourself to be lucid during nightmares. In part this is why lucidity is so well regarded. Several gadgets have been devised to encourage lucidity. They may flash or flicker in order to rouse dreamers sufficiently for them to become lucid without actually waking up. However, there are things that you can do yourself to induce lucidity if you have a nightmare:

- Set an alarm to go off every 80 minutes at the start of your night's sleep. This will prevent REM sleep and reduce your chance of nightmares.
- Listen to very relaxing music or sounds, such as the calls of whales or the sound of water, as you drift off to sleep. These may become incorporated into dream content in a pleasant way.

Case Study

"I am being chased by the most horrible demon. I am running away from it on a road that is surrounded by hedges. As I look at the hedges, I realize they are made of dismembered bodies. The thing that is chasing me has spun a web of some kind and I find myself trapped in it. I suddenly realize I am dreaming, but I cannot move. I know this isn't real, but I can do nothing to stop the demon coming to get me. As it reaches me, hand open, I wake up terrified."

—Male student, 24 years of age

Children's Nightmares

Do you remember having a nightmare as a child, and how hard it was to accept that it wasn't real? Perhaps you woke up just before a wild animal sunk its great teeth into you. Parents around the world comfort their children by telling them it was just a dream. Learning that there is a world that is real and one that is not is one of the most forgettable facts about nightmares and dreaming. As adults we don't recall this transition, but we may remember how terrifying childhood nightmares can be if we had them.

There are peak ages when nightmares occur. The first peak is around the age of five and the next is during late adolescence. This is, of course, a generalized picture based on large amounts of data. Every child develops at his or her own rate and has nightmares differently. As is the case when treating adults, an approach that works for one child may not suit another.

Fierce animals commonly feature in children's nightmares.

How can I minimize my child's distress after a nightmare?

- Encourage your child to tell you the nightmare.
- Talk to the part of the nightmare that is scary for the child and tell it to "Go away."
- Be prepared to spend some time comforting your child. Don't minimize his or her fear and distress.
- Explain what a dream is.
- Reassure your child that you are close by.
- If nightmares are occurring frequently, encourage a young child to use a security object, such as a blanket, when awake. This will bring comfort.
- Finally we should not forget that children still have the wonderful ability to think magically. They believe in miracles, the tooth fairy, and all manner of imaginary characters. You can use the positive figments of a child's imagination to counteract their night terrors.

How to help children who have nightmares: the four Rs

Alan Seigel and Kelly Bulkeley, prominent dream researchers, have looked at ways of bringing relief to children who experience nightmares—the four Rs:

1. *Reassurance* Tell the child that everything is OK. Comfort them.

2. *Rescripting* Work with the child to change the nightmare into a positive dream experience.

3. *Rehearsal* Help the child to rehearse the new dream as often as possible.

4. *Resolution* Help the child to develop a "magical tool box" for bad dreams, so that he or she knows what's best to do if the nightmare recurs.

Another prominent researcher in this field, Patricia Garfield, points out that children only think in terms of good dreams and bad dreams, so we should keep it simple both in terms of the language we use and the way the four Rs are applied. Make it as much fun as possible.

What are children's nightmares about?

The monster under the bed is the classic child's nightmare. The boy or girl will wake up afraid that something horrible is going to get them. The child won't know what it is, but may say it's a bad man, a monster, or an animal that he or she is afraid of while awake. Children may also have nightmares that a parent or someone close to them has gone away and left them. Psychologists see these as examples of separation anxiety, which is a common stage in child development.

What is normal?

Approximately 40 percent of children between the ages of 5 and 12 have occasional nightmares. Quite often the child does not remember what the nightmare was about, but he or she will wake up distressed and be afraid to go back to sleep. Young children in particular may not be able to understand the difference between dreaming and reality.

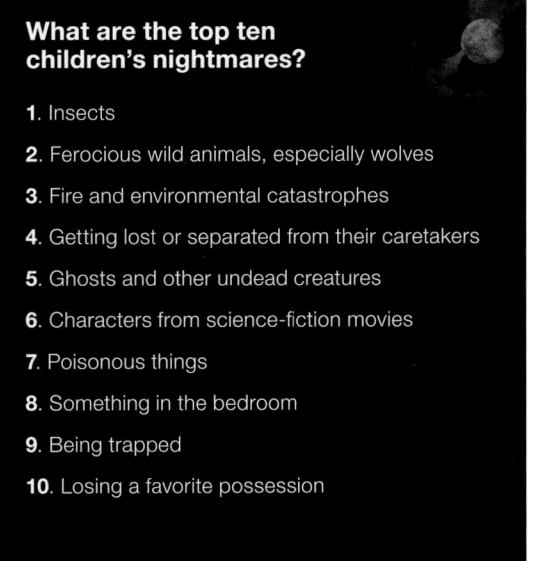

What are the top ten children's nightmares?

1. Insects

2. Ferocious wild animals, especially wolves

3. Fire and environmental catastrophes

4. Getting lost or separated from their caretakers

5. Ghosts and other undead creatures

6. Characters from science-fiction movies

7. Poisonous things

8. Something in the bedroom

9. Being trapped

10. Losing a favorite possession

Nightmare Symbols & Themes

The more you are able to decipher your nightmares and their symbolic language, the more open you will be to the messages these dreams contain. Remember that they are just that: dreams. They are not real.

Researcher Jeremy Taylor, a founding member of the International Association for the Study of Dreams, suggests that every dream we have, no matter how unpleasant, provides the blueprint for a deeper understanding of the self. In other words, nightmares are helpful—once we give our attention to this kind of dream, it will loosen its hold on us and become less frequent. Try to enjoy the tasks suggested to you by your nightmares. These dreams are ultimately beneficial, despite the discomfort you undergo while having them.

What Is Your Nightmare Telling You?

Through the unpleasantness of the experience, nightmares awaken us to the alarm call produced by our mind to change ourselves for the better. Each symbol, animal, place, or event that is presented can take us farther down the road to self-understanding and bring us closer to a balanced life.

The Shadow

Of all the nightmarish characters, the shadow is the most frequent visitor to our dreams. He is also the most written about. This shady character takes many forms, but you'll know him by the feelings of fear and suspicion he engenders. He may be a robber or a villain. Worst of all, he may be someone you know and love. If one of your dream characters is frightening you or acting in a way that you believe is immoral, you can be sure that the shadow is at large.

How dream analysts interpret it We all have a shadow self, and he comes into his own in our nightmares. This is the part of ourselves that we don't like or can't accept. It may be how you behave sometimes or how you feel, or it may lie in the thoughts you have about other people. Carl Jung (see pages 14–15 of Dreams) believed that it is part of our life's work to face up to our shadow self and overcome it. This doesn't mean you should eliminate your dark side, even if this were possible, but rather that you should acknowledge it. The shadow is put in his rightful place when you accept, like everyone else in the world, that you have good and also less good qualities. He brings fear to our nightmares because we don't want to know about the unpleasant parts of ourselves. If you embrace the shadow, you remove his power, and he won't come knocking on your dreams.

Try this to gain insight If you have a shadow dream, ask yourself the following:

1. Reflect carefully on the dream while you are awake.
2. Identify the characteristics of this particular shadow. Was he, for example, envious, lazy, greedy, spiteful, or mean?
3. Acknowledge that these characteristics are part of you. Write down examples of where you have shown each one in your daily life.
4. Make the decision not to give yourself a hard time. Instead, watch for these characteristics and the next time they emerge, refuse to act on your savage impulses.

Symbolizes dark, unconscious self-representation

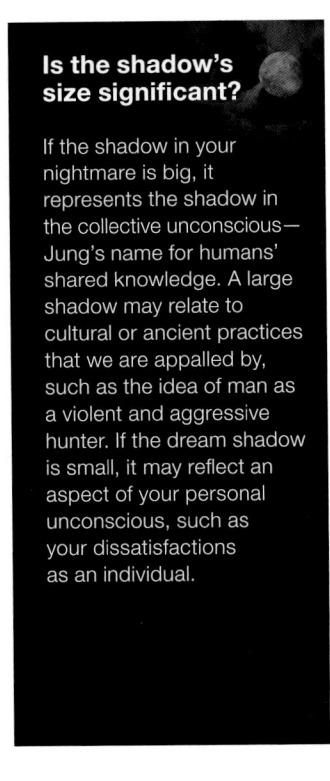

Is the shadow's size significant?

If the shadow in your nightmare is big, it represents the shadow in the collective unconscious—Jung's name for humans' shared knowledge. A large shadow may relate to cultural or ancient practices that we are appalled by, such as the idea of man as a violent and aggressive hunter. If the dream shadow is small, it may reflect an aspect of your personal unconscious, such as your dissatisfactions as an individual.

The Evil Woman

Like the shadow, the evil woman regularly stalks our dreams. She is his feminine flip side. Just like him, she takes on many different guises. She may be modeled on the wicked witch of Western culture, or on the female jinni from Hinduism. Whatever her form, you are unlikely to recognize her because she is almost always a stranger. The evil woman embodies those parts of ourselves that are destructive and that erode emotional balance and well-being.

How dream analysts interpret it Jung believed that none of us is able to escape the influence of the dark forces in our psyche, but that we should work hard to accept them and keep them in check. He saw the evil woman as that part of the anima (see page 38 of Dreams) that must be brought under control so that the power of femininity can be used positively. A dream of the evil woman can be terrifying! Evil is, after all, a very strong word. However, it's important to remember that her power is inflated. She appears with great force to get our attention, so that we will start the valuable work of defusing her.

Freud (see pages 12–13 of Dreams) was never surprised by evil, whether it took a male or female form. He saw dreams that contained nasty, shadowlike figures as good for our health. He reasoned that the negative energy produced by the evil woman, or rather our self at its most extreme and twisted, has to be expressed somehow. According to Freud, if the evil woman gets to dance in our dreams, she will be easier to keep hidden when we are awake.

Questions to ask yourself Who is the evil woman in your dream? To explore what she may mean, ask yourself the questions below. To make the process meaningful, it's important to be honest when you answer.

1. Whom does she remind me of?
2. Which of this person's waking characteristics annoy or irritate me?
3. Why is this exactly? Which part of me is threatened by these characteristics?

Symbolizes self-destructive forces, waking ethics

How common are evil woman dreams?

An evil female presence is often reported during sleep paralysis (see page 26). This phenomenon, which more than half of us experience at least once in our lives, is reported throughout history and across cultures. The woman who appears is known by various names, including the Old Hag in Canada and the Trampling Ogress in France. If you have sleep paralysis without understanding its physical effects, you may believe you have seen a ghost.

The Shape-Shifter

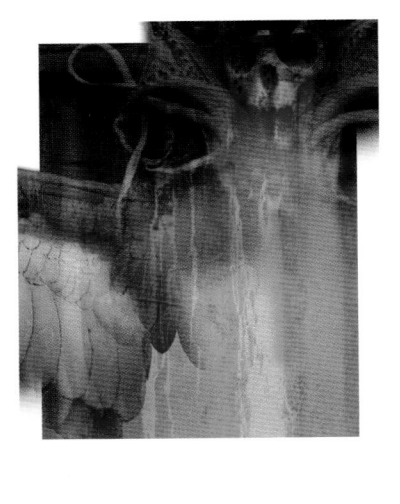

This type of nightmare demonstrates our incredible adaptability to shift into, and make the best of, every situation. The slippery little critters in our dreams can be horribly subtle. One minute you may be fighting with your boyfriend, the next minute you notice something odd about his shoes or that he's wearing glasses, and it dawns on you that he's your father. Why does your old teacher look so much like your wife? When the shape-shifter is doing his work, you can't be too sure of anything.

How dream analysts interpret it Jung maintained that every character in a dream reflects a part of the dreamer's psyche. Shape-shifter dreams can be visual metaphors for passing knowledge from one state of our consciousness into another. A shape-shift from the animus (see page 39 of Dreams) to the shadow may reflect the moment when you realize that someone close to you is not trustworthy. Shape-shifting is also a great exploration tool. We are all connected to a universal store of memory, and changing our appearance allows us to broaden our experience. If you encourage shape-shifting in your dreams (see below), you will gain insight into all types of existence.

Freud related shape-shifting to his theory of the three levels of personality: the id, the ego, and the superego (see pages 12–13 of Dreams). If you dream of an unruly child, you're regressing and connecting with a less mature version of yourself. If the child becomes an adult who is approachable and pleasant, you are moving toward a more mature stage of development.

Try this to gain insight A shape-shifting dream is an excellent choice for incubation (see pages 30–31 of Dreams). Have you ever wondered what it is like to be a member of the opposite sex or a particular type of animal? If you incubate successfully, you can open yourself to a range of other lives. Your choice of character will tell you something about your needs. If you choose to incubate a child, it may indicate that you want some freedom from responsibility. If you incubate a heroic character, you may be looking for adventure.

Symbolizes the ability to adapt, experiencing life from different perspectives

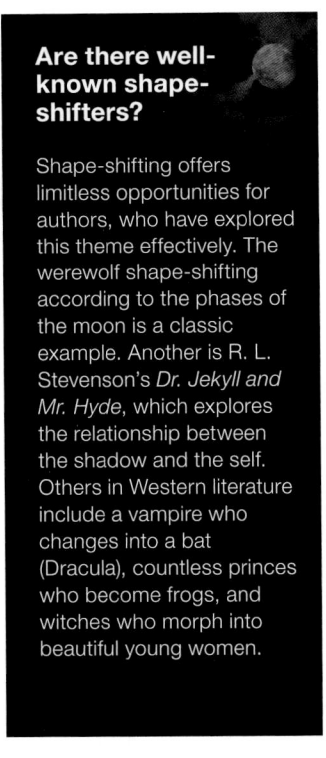

Are there well-known shape-shifters?

Shape-shifting offers limitless opportunities for authors, who have explored this theme effectively. The werewolf shape-shifting according to the phases of the moon is a classic example. Another is R. L. Stevenson's *Dr. Jekyll and Mr. Hyde*, which explores the relationship between the shadow and the self. Others in Western literature include a vampire who changes into a bat (Dracula), countless princes who become frogs, and witches who morph into beautiful young women.

The Prostitute

This archetype describes the way we sell ourselves for material gain at the expense of our spiritual well-being. The prostitute may appear in your nightmares as male or female. If female, you should pay attention to the way feminine traits are used in your life, by you or someone you know, to get what is wanted. If the gigolo appears, pay attention to masculine traits, which may be used by someone of either sex to sell out. Essentially, this symbol sends out the message that self-empowerment comes a poor second to material goods, ways of behaving, and thought processes, which although expedient, do your true self no favors.

How dream analysts interpret it The prostitute archetype is everywhere in today's society, which often celebrates the pursuit of power and material success. However, the appearance of this character in a dream, or even in a nightmare, may be viewed positively. Jung would say it indicated that spiritual progress, or the journey toward individuation, is well under way. The prostitute prompts you to question if you are still being propelled by materialism or self-will. People who have faith in themselves, or in the powers of the universe, don't need to sacrifice what they know is right. This is one of the best nightmares you can have, and it's an important one. When the prostitute sounds the siren, take action immediately.

Questions to ask yourself To make the most of this special dream symbol, ask yourself where in your life the symbol applies. Start off by asking the two questions below. It can be helpful to apply these separately to your relationships (sexual and otherwise), your work life, and your health.
1. Where in my life do I have a price?
2. Where in my life can I be used?

Symbolizes lack of faith, threats to survival, selling the soul

How can I escape this nightmare?

In the 30 minutes you set aside each day (see page 27 of Dreams), foster the feeling that everything you need will be provided. Tell yourself that there is nothing in life for which you should put aside your principles. We routinely override them when we don't believe our needs will be met. Dream therapist Caroline Myss says that to relinquish the prostitute we need to develop faith. Think about all the things we can sell, as well as sex, that cost us more than we get in return: our energy, time, dignity, integrity, and morality.

The Bully

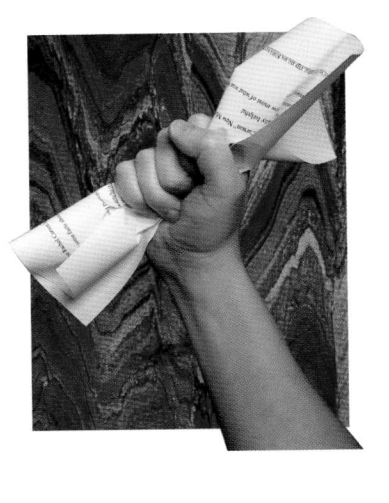

This character is usually male and will manifest himself in a nightmare as a powerful, maybe overbearing, energy. Sometimes he's a typical thug, who stops the dream from feeling free by intimidating the other characters and being verbally or physically abusive. In other cases this archetype may be present as a symbolic threat or an underlying sense of unease. You might, for example, be scared in a nightmare that someone's big brother is going to get you if you stand up for yourself. The bully is very often a patchwork of all the negative thoughts you have about yourself, stitched together to make a monster.

How dream analysts interpret it The bully can suggest an overinflated ego, belonging to someone in our lives who thinks it's possible to get what he or she wants by intimidation. But we know that the driving force behind a bully is fear. A bully pretends to be in control to mask feelings of inferiority and cowardice. In this sense the archetype represents the opposite of its outward appearance. It comes to your nightmares on a wave of terror. The more aggressive your bully, the more he is afraid.

Dream therapist Caroline Myss tells us not to take the bully at face value by explaining that the bully in a nightmare is an aspect of the dreamer. So if you have this dream, ask yourself how you are dishonoring your spirit. Are you bullying yourself out of taking the correct course of action because you are afraid? The story line of the dream and the setting will help you understand how you are doing yourself harm.

Questions to ask yourself To understand why the bully is appearing in your dreams, ask yourself:
1. Is this character representative of someone I know or used to know, who is a bully? Or does it refer to a real experience of bullying, either happening now or in the past?
2. Am I behaving like a victim? Where do I need to stand up for myself more?
3. Which parts of my thinking do I feel bullied by?

Symbolizes intimidation, active superego

What is an example of the bully?

The Harry Potter books by J. K. Rowling can be used to illustrate Jung's idea that the psyche is made up of distinct characters that create a network of complex relationships. Harry is the hero and Voldemort is the shadow with shape-shifter aspects. The Dementors represent the power of negative thought to suck the soul dry. The Malfoy family represents the bully at various stages of development, and Hogwarts, Harry's school, represents the self and the absolute limitlessness of human potential.

The Trickster

This archetype represents the part of every person that is rebellious. It is the side of human nature that doesn't want to change. The trickster will set out to sabotage fruitful endeavors or halt development that may be psychologically painful. Like the bully, this character has no moral code. He doesn't care how he hurts you, thinks nothing of ridiculing you for your good intentions, and revels in malicious gossip. The jester, or joker, who uses humor to make light of bad situations, represents the trickster's positive side. However, in both his aspects, the main function of this character is to prevent you from moving forward and becoming a better person.

How dream analysts interpret it The trickster is the psychic opposite of the part of ourselves that we can trust. It is the side of us that doesn't care about the consequences of what we say or do to other people. This immature character appears in your dreams so that when you are awake you are better able to resist the temptation to cause mischief. Do you find life a little dull sometimes? Do you to cause a little chaos?

Remember that some of the most hurtful words are delivered as jokes. Engaging with the trickster in your dreams will encourage you to control your impulses in this direction and become more sure of yourself. The trickster, through all his attempts to destabilize, helps us to trust ourselves.

Questions to ask yourself The trickster may appear in a deed rather than as a person. Consider the factors in your dreams that prevent you from getting to where you want to go.
1. Do cars break down, travel plans go wrong, or are you late because of an incident blocking you, such as a broken bridge? This is the trickster in action.
2. If you have trickster dreams, ask yourself why you are trying to sabotage yourself, whether in a relationship, at work, or in any other way.
3. If your dream involves a hitch in travel plans, for example, look at the part of the journey the trickster is interrupting and ask why you are reluctant to go any farther.

Symbolizes immaturity, selfishness, lack of psychological development

How do I work with the trickster?

It's important to make friends with this dream symbol. The trickster can be destructive, but he is not wholly bad. Once acknowledged and recognized, his energy can be transformed into the part of us that is fun and spontaneous, and that is willing to take appropriate risks. Try working with this character using some of the suggestions on pages 28–29 of Dreams.

The Demon/Devil

The devil appears in some of our most hair-raising nightmares. The meaning of this menacing creature can be elusive, but it is never easy. Whether he's a demon or the devil himself, this symbol is the manifestation of everything that the dreamer considers to be bad or evil. Unlike other nightmarish characters, he is usually inhuman, not only in appearance but also in the terror he brings. Nothing human, however wicked, could scare you this much. A demon or devil in your dream may be symbolic of illness or misfortune. He may highlight addictive tendencies or malicious intent. The interpretation of this dark force will depend upon your particular associations with the symbol.

How dream analysts interpret it The devil in our nightmares is indicative of the spiritual struggle that we all face at various times in our lives, perhaps when we know we are behaving badly or going against our beliefs. It also represents the parts of our psyche that have been around for the longest, and should be discarded. The devil's message may be that you need to evolve. He can also embody temptation. Jung's journey toward individuation is littered with invitations to take the wrong path. It is up to you, the dreamer, whether you succumb. You may, for example, be attracted to someone who is unavailable. The attraction is normal; acting on it isn't.

Projection, one of Freud's defense mechanisms, may be at work here. Without realizing it, we use this mechanism to project onto other people emotions or problems we don't want to admit are our own. Is there an event buried in your memory that you cannot put a name to, which you have either forgotten or repressed in your waking life? The devil or demons can appear as amalgamations of everything that we think is safest to avoid.

Questions to ask yourself If the devil has ever appeared in your nightmares, ask yourself the following three questions:
1. What is there in my waking life that is so terrible I can't bear to look at it?
2. Is there evidence of addictive behavior in any area of my life? What about in the lives of the people close to me?
3. If this character was someone I knew, who would it be?

Symbolizes repression, addiction, malicious intent

Who is the devil at the end of the bed?

In about 3 percent of recorded incidences of sleep paralysis (see page 24), the dreamer sees a devilish figure in his or her bedroom. The devil in these cases often fits a biblical description, or a Hollywood one. When the sighting has occurred outside of Western culture, however, the description tallies with the dominant cultural image of demons. Even though these images appear extraordinarily real, this suggests that they are in fact constructed by the dreamer's imagination.

The Vampire

The vampire is a well-known shady figure from Transylvanian folklore. He will come to your dreams cloaked in mystery, yet for all his glamour, he is essentially a parasite. This character can live only by draining the life force of others. If he fails to feed, he will become weak. Vampires are too clever to reveal their intentions upfront. Exuding magnificent eroticism, they use their ability to hypnotize and shape-shift to get what they require. There is little about this player that is real. The vampire is dangerous because he feeds off your illusions.

How dream analysts interpret it The vampire may appear in your dreams as an aspect of your shadow self. As such, the vampire may indicate that one aspect of your personality is taking over or living off the other parts. In more recent writing by dream theorists, this archetype has been associated with codependency. Codependency is a form of addiction, whereby the drug is the drama of another person. This condition usually occurs in people from a dysfunctional family who have already witnessed addictive behavior. If you are codependent, you will focus obsessively on someone else at the expense of yourself. Feeding in this way, as the vampire knows, is a great way of avoiding our own problems.

Freud believed that the vampire embodies the fascination we all have with death and its inevitability. By dreaming of vampires, which are immortal, we successfully avoid our fears and fulfill our wish to live forever, whatever the cost to others. Alternatively, a vampire dream can reflect a desire for sex without emotion. A vampire simply devours the object of its desire, then leaves. Freud talked only about sexual vampirism, but when working with this symbol, you may find it useful to consider its emotional equivalent.

Questions to ask yourself The appearance of this archetype can indicate a destructive relationship. If this is true in your case, you can help yourself by asking the following:
1. Who do I feel is sucking me dry?
2. Why am I hypnotized by this relationship?
3. What would happen if I told this person to stop?

Symbolizes dependency on others, sexual magnetism, illusion

Are you the vampire or its victim?

Vampirism can be a metaphor for the use one person makes of another for his or her own ends. This may be emotional or sexual, or relate to any aspect of the person. You might dream of the vampire if you are its metaphorical victim. In this case the vampire would reflect your diminished sense of who you are and the feeling you have of feeding someone else's needs rather than your own. The vampire in your life may pretend to act with concern for your welfare, but he or she will be very needy or destructive.

Malformed Babies or Animals

A malformed and vulnerable creature is perhaps the most common nightmare symbol. What makes this nightmare especially unpleasant is that the dreamer may witness the pain of the animal or baby but be powerless to help. The root cause may be hurt feelings that the dreamer finds difficult to verbalize. Another interpretation of this symbol is as an expression of ideas that are at a very early stage in their development and that, in their current form, will fail to reach fruition. Similarly, it can refer to embryonic aspects of the self that the dreamer is struggling to manifest appropriately while awake. If you have a nightmare in which you are swimming among thousands of oversized tadpoles, for example, the suggestion is that your emotions (the water) are immature (the infant frogs).

How dream analysts interpret it Jung's dream theory allows you to explore your dreams in relation to what is happening in your life now and in relation to what is taking place in your psyche from a broader perspective—the part of you that connects to the collective unconscious. Taking the wider view, you might see a dream of mutilated babies or animals as a reminder that we are each a miracle of nature. To be born perfectly formed is an astonishing outcome and one that we often take for granted.

Dreams of animals with abnormalities are commonly reported by people who have suffered abuse. These nightmares can be unpleasant but can be viewed positively if the dreamer tries to look after the animal and soothe its distress. This shows that the abused person is ready to self-care. The malformed animal is a visual manifestation of the injured part of the dreamer.

Try this to gain insight If a child appears in your dreams and it is hurt, crying, or wounded in some way, ask yourself:

1. Has the child appeared before? Check your journal and see what state it was in. A change will help you review progress.
2. Does anyone you know need care? The dream may be about that person. Or ask yourself if you have any suppressed hurt feelings. If so, think about how to dispel them in waking life. Sometimes just admitting to them stops the nightmare.

Symbolizes primitive parts of the self, new ideas or projects that need more thought, unexpressed hurts

What does a difficult birth in a nightmare symbolize?

If the dreamer is pregnant or is about to become a father, a dream of a malformed baby can symbolize his or her fears about the child and the coming birth. Anxiety dreams are very common among prospective parents. In less literal cases, a difficult birth in a dream can correspond with an emerging idea or problem. In a nightmare a deformity may be found in a baby just after it is born. This suggests that a project requires a great deal more development.

The Addict

This nightmare character is an aspect of the shadow. The addict may be mood-altered by alcohol or drugs, food, shopping, sex, money, or work. Whatever the addiction, the dreaming mind knows it is harmful and reflects this by giving the addict an unpleasant, disturbing appearance. If it is you, the dreamer, who is inebriated, you may find yourself unable to carry out a required action because of your condition. The addict is the saboteur—the part of you that prevents the emergence of your true self.

How dream analysts interpret it Jung took a positive view of human nature. For him, this symbol represents something that is blocking us from being our authentic selves. We all need at times to avoid how we feel, and the addict reflects this. The addict runs from pain, won't even acknowledge it, and keeps running. By refusing to deal with the reality of life, he or she takes any route to avoid responsibility. This archetype, therefore, suggests a willingness to compromise integrity and honesty, when the dreamer or another dream character allows addictive distractions to override what he or she ought to be focusing on. If you have this nightmare, work with it as soon as you can, before the addictive behavior affects an important waking-life situation.

Have you ever tried to give up an addiction? If you have ever been a smoker, for example, and stopped, you may have had dreams in which you smoked. Researchers call dreams like this absent-minded transgressions. A recovering addict will try all day not to think about smoking or using another drug, but his or her desire is allowed satisfaction in the safe world of dreams.

Questions to ask yourself This can be one of the most illuminating dream symbols if you dare to interpret it honestly. Start by asking the following questions of the addict or yourself:
1. Why is this person (or you) inebriated or high?
2. What is this person avoiding in life by behaving in this way?
3. What would you say if you could tell this person how to face this issue? You may want to enter into a dialogue with the wise old woman to see what she says (see page 45 of Dreams).

Symbolizes self-destruction, immaturity, sabotage, avoidance of a waking issue

How can I interpret relapse dreams?

Research into the dreams of people recovering from addictive behavior in the U.K., in 1995, found that relapse dreams are a part of recovery. There were differences between alcoholics and opiate users. Alcoholics drank in nightmares and suffered the consequences, but opiate users are prevented from using drugs. The nightmare centers around getting the drug, but the dreamer wakes before using. Recovering addicts should talk to someone they trust about their relapse dreams.

Injured Animals

Injured animals often feature in the nightmares of men and women who have been ill-treated. In these instances the animal reflects the dreamer's feelings of woundedness or hurt. An exception would be if the dreamer were pregnant, in which case an injured animal would express her anxiety about becoming a parent. Or the dreamer may have strong associations with animals, perhaps because of the nature of his or her job. Nearly always, however, this imagery is a symbol of the dreamer's own emotional pain. If you have this nightmare as a consequence of physical or sexual abuse, you must find professional support. Dream work in this area is highly specialized and should not be attempted without the guidance of a qualified therapist.

How dream analysts interpret it Jung believed that wounded animals reflect parts of the psyche that are underdeveloped and emotionally damaged. If you have this dream, the nature of the animals and the way in which they are hurt should be explored to fully understand the meaning behind the dream. According to Jung, different animals have different energies. The bear is associated with strength and the dog with loyalty. So if you dream of a wounded dog, your "injury" most likely relates to friendship. Perhaps someone close to you has been disloyal. Your unconscious is helping by applying your raw emotion to a dog, an animal known for its devotion, which you can identify with easily.

Another way of looking at this dream is as a projection of pain we don't want to own or accept. We use the defense mechanism of projection, identified by Freud, to protect ourselves. Because the truth is too painful, the dreamer may transfer hurt on to an animal. This allows the dreamer to experience feelings of sadness in a way that isn't harmful or overwhelming.

Questions to ask yourself These dreams are not easy to work with, but the results make the process worthwhile. If you have had a nightmare about injured animal, ask yourself:

1. If I was this animal, which part of my life would this dream reflect?
2. Which part of me feels as though it has been treated like an animal?

Symbolizes woundedness, hurt feelings, projection

Is concern for animals a factor?

A study by Jacquie Lewis, at the Saybrook Graduate School in San Francisco, focused on the dreams of animal rights activists in order to test the idea that only children dream about animals. She found that animals appeared in 29.7 percent of 284 dreams. This compares with data collected by Hall and Van de Castle in 1966, which found animals in only 4 percent of dreams. Lewis concluded that if people have an emotional connection with animals, they are more likely to visualize them while they are dreaming.

Swarms

Swarms are the dark masses that hover in the background until the dreamer realizes what they are and shudders in disgust. At this point the swarm may come rapidly to the forefront. Locusts, wasps, mosquitoes, bats, cockroaches, and flies have all been mentioned in dream reports. Flies are particularly common because they are associated with dirt and disease. If a nightmarish swarm invades your dreams, it may represent your most negative thoughts. Alternatively, it may suggest someone you know that you find repulsive.

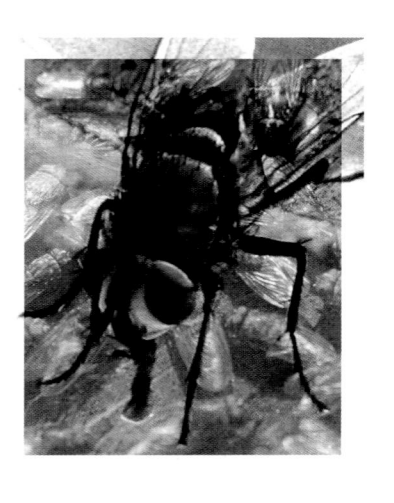

How dream analysts interpret it Swarms can be unpleasant and disturbing. They belong to our shadow-self. Jung believed they represented the outlying parts of our consciousness that we don't want to acknowledge. The feelings of disgust that the swarm evokes and the fear make the dreamer want to run a mile. Freud, also saw swarms as revolting collections of thoughts and feelings that have been repressed by the dreamer. The dark forces in a swarm are so reviled, they cannot be expressed as a regular nightmare image, not even a monster or demon.

To find the meaning of a swarm, Freud asked the dreamer to associate with the name of the particular insect (see page 15 for an explanation of Freud's method). Both Freud and Jung believed that exploring a swarm through its associations was the best way to unravel its meaning. Slugs, for example, suggest lethargy. If your nightmare is bulging with these slimy creatures, you may be expressing a violent dislike of sluggish behavior.

Try this to gain insight The revulsion you feel in this dream, followed by a desire to escape, are important. The feelings evoked by a symbol, rather than the symbol itself, are key to a dream's interpretation. Start exploring with this exercise:

1. Ask if there is a person, place, or situation that you feel you cannot escape. Nightmares in this category are often recalled with expressions such as, "[He or she] was all over me."
2. Once you have identified the person or situation that is your swarm, honor the nightmare. Think about how to disengage from your swarm, and carry out your plan immediately.

Symbolizes revulsion, escape, negative thinking

What does a swarm mean in children's nightmares?

Insects quite often appear in children's nightmares. They may wake up very distressed because a huge insect appeared in their dream and was trying to eat them. The meaning of this dream is usually that something in waking life is bugging the child. The size of the insect may reflect the size of the worry. The same interpretation often holds true for adult nightmares, too.

Insects

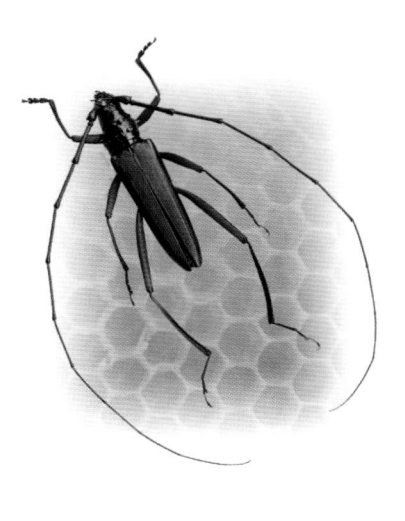

A dream of insects doesn't have to mean a swarm. An entire dream may be taken up in avoiding one very nasty grasshopper or in focusing on the damage it wreaks. When working closely with a dream of this kind, the key is to explore what your chosen insect represents in your case. A more general interpretation is that insects reflect some kind of aggravation, such as they so often cause in real life. Very few people actively like them. If it is life-size, you feel in control of the issue it represents. If, however, the insect is monstrously large, your problem is overwhelming.

How dream analysts interpret it We are instinctively repelled by the strangeness of insects. However, if we look at an insect objectively, we discover that it is quite beautiful. Your nightmare may be the psyche telling you not to accept something at face value, but to look deeper. Once we override the urge to escape, we can appreciate the beauty in what we previously saw as ugly.

Jung regarded insects as a reflection of underdeveloped areas of the psyche and looked for specific meaning in the dreamer's choice of insect. The wood louse, for example, is typically insectlike in its lack of autonomy. It survives by reacting to its body temperature and moving to light or shade accordingly. A wood louse in a nightmare may, therefore, refer to the part of the dreamer that acts because it cannot think. The dream's message would be to become more aware of your actions.

Try this to gain insight To find out whether the insect in your nightmare is bringing you a message, try this:
1. Make two columns in your journal, one headed Positives and the other headed Negatives.
2. Write down all the attributes of your insect that you can think of, placing each in the appropriate column.
3. Now re-enter the dream and ask the insect to talk to you. Ask it what it has to say.
4. Write down its message and how it applies to your life or someone in your life.
5. Finally, ask yourself which of the insect's positive attributes you have or would like to have.

Symbolizes face-value judgments, worries, hidden beauty

Repulsive insects or bearers of wisdom?

Many insects live on dead or rotting meat, and in myth they are allowed to go to the underworld and to return with knowledge. The underworld can be regarded as symbolic of the unconscious part of your psyche. Put instinct aside for a few minutes and engage with your dream insects, and you may learn something. You could try a Gestalt-type role-play (see pages 18–19 of Dreams) or make them the focus of a meditation. Ask them why they are here, and listen to their reply.

Imaginary Creatures

Your dreaming mind puts no limits on your creations, which leads to some terrifying creatures. Special effects in movies and the sophisticated imagery of computer games can spark your imagination and help shape your fantastical visions. Every imaginary creature, however, has its basis in truth or myth. Mythical creatures have always been popular in nightmares (see box right). Some are hybrid: part animal, part human. Like swarms and insects, when they appear in a nightmare, they disgust you and trigger your flight response. The bigger they are, the more important the issue or transition will be in your waking life.

How dream analysts interpret it We grow up surrounded by story and myth and, as adults, we use these templates unconsciously to help understand the world. Jung responded to dreams of mythical creatures by encouraging the dreamer to explore the stories surrounding them. If you have a nightmare of an imaginary creature, Jung would tell you to look up its mythical history to discover where you need to develop in waking life. Jung used imaginary creatures extensively to understand his psyche and journey toward individuation. In his *Red Book*, published for the first time in 2009, he drew many of his visions, including sea monsters and snakes with the tree of life in their mouths. He described these drawings as "cryptograms of myself—that appear to me each day."

Try this to gain insight Have you dreamed of an imaginary creature? If so, you may want to reflect on the movies you've been watching. These visions are now likely to appear as residue from your day. Having said that, all dreams show us our potential for imagination and creativity. To honor this nightmare, draw the mythical creature you saw in as much detail as you remember. Focus on its complexity and reflect on which aspects of it you are particularly drawn to. Does your creature have wings? If so, you may need to fly away from something. Is it magical? If so, ask yourself if you have any talents that you need to develop. Is it strong? This may be a reflection of your own inner strength.

Symbolizes imagination, ancient archetypal knowledge

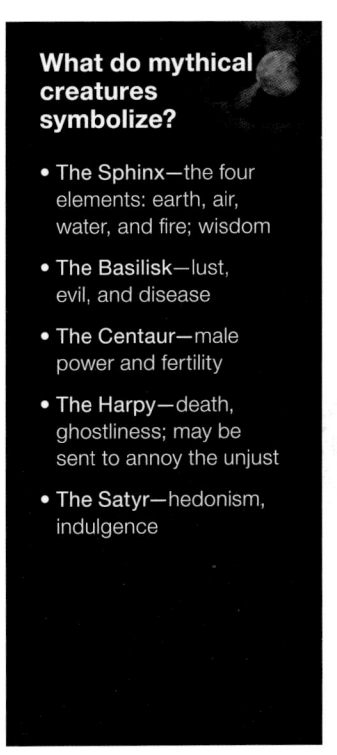

What do mythical creatures symbolize?

- The Sphinx—the four elements: earth, air, water, and fire; wisdom

- The Basilisk—lust, evil, and disease

- The Centaur—male power and fertility

- The Harpy—death, ghostliness; may be sent to annoy the unjust

- The Satyr—hedonism, indulgence

The Spider

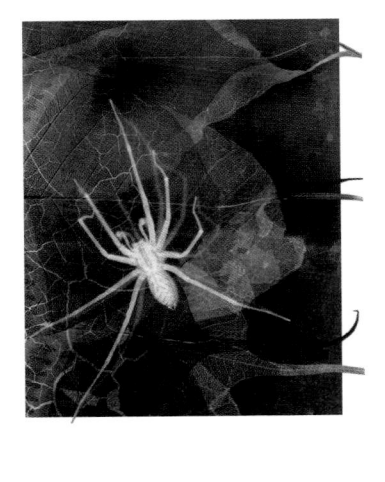

Spiders, the spinners of webs, can be venomous. Do you scream when you see one in the bath? Fear of spiders is one of the most commonly reported phobias. For someone with arachnophobia, spiders are obvious creatures to appear in a nightmare. But these hardworking creatures don't deserve their bad press. The Scottish king Robert the Bruce was famously encouraged to continue his fight against the English after watching a spider toil patiently to finish its web. Black widows, a name also given to female murderers, stick more closely to the nightmare theme by insisting on eating the male after mating.

How dream analysts interpret it For Jung, the spider was symbolic of the great mother in her devouring form. The great mother is the weaver of destiny. She controls not only the fate of the planet but also our individual fortunes. If this archetype appears in your nightmare, your destiny is being challenged or is changing its route. This is your alarm call. The importance of the decision you face, which will alter your future forever, is apparent by the extreme feelings that accompany the nightmare. A spider dream is telling you to look at where you are in the web of life. Who or what are you are thinking of devouring?

Freud had a lot to say about spiders. For him, they represented female genitalia. A scary spider would suggest that the dreamer is frightened of women. He also linked spiders with pregnancy and believed that women who dreamed of spiders were expressing a wish for children.

Questions to ask yourself This powerful dream image can appear at important times in a dreamer's life. If you dream of a spider, ask the following:
1. How old am I? What is expected of me at this age?
2. Is this a transitional point in my life? If so, how can I honor that?
3. Have I woven a complicated web somewhere?
4. Is this complication necessary?

Symbolizes female energy, the great mother, life's journey

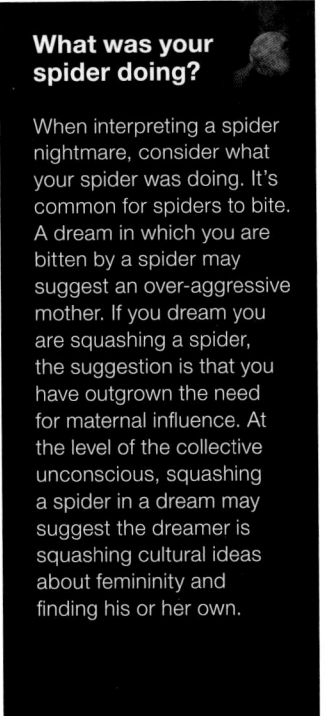

What was your spider doing?

When interpreting a spider nightmare, consider what your spider was doing. It's common for spiders to bite. A dream in which you are bitten by a spider may suggest an over-aggressive mother. If you dream you are squashing a spider, the suggestion is that you have outgrown the need for maternal influence. At the level of the collective unconscious, squashing a spider in a dream may suggest the dreamer is squashing cultural ideas about femininity and finding his or her own.

The Hyena

As with other animal symbols, the appearance of the hyena in a nightmare may be a literal representation of what we commonly associate with this animal during waking life. The hyena is a scavenger. It lives off the misfortune of others, and, like the vulture, it quickly identifies the weak and vulnerable. Hyenas are motivated by a survival instinct. They are killing machines. Their arch enemy is the lion.

How dream analysts interpret it Inside us all is a part, associated with the shadow, that will survive at any cost. The hyena is a manifestation of those behaviors that are the opposite of what you would expect from an honorable person. This creature is known for its sneakiness and opportunism. These are not the qualities of someone who acts responsibly. The hyena is associated with gluttony, uncleanliness, and cowardice. Because it is prepared to do whatever is necessary to get by, it may also be viewed as the animal form of the prostitute (see page 41). If you dream of a hyena, there is a powerful negative force in your life that must be addressed. Does your dream hyena resemble someone you know?

Questions to ask yourself Thankfully, this is a rare dream. If you ever experience it, you need to consider how low your behavior has become for the purposes of survival, as you perceive it. Ask yourself the following:
1. In which area of my life do I feel like a scavenger?
2. If this symbol is not representing me, then who is it representing?
3. How can I satisfy the part of myself that feels as if it is scavenging for morsels to survive?
4. Alternatively, who is scavenging for morsels from me?

Symbolizes gluttony, mimicry, unevolved parts of the self

Can we learn from the hyena?

Like flies, hyenas live off the dead, so they have access to their souls and to the underworld. This association opens the way for us to use the hyena positively. The underworld can be seen as a symbol of our unconscious mind. It exists, but we are not aware of it. What was your hyena eating; which part of you is threatened by a scavenger? The threat may be a person, place, or an aspect of yourself. Interpretation helps you make conscious previously hidden knowledge.

The Lion

The lion makes quite frequent visits to our nightmares, especially in chasing mode. Most people have imagined being caught and ripped apart by a raging lion. Symbolically, this regal creature represents loyalty and pride. In a nightmare its appearance may suggest that the dreamer has acted without dignity. Alternatively, it may suggest a need for the dreamer to rule his or her own domain, because lions are known for being territorial. The lion has religious connotations for some. In a nightmare it might appear as the devil in disguise.

How dream analysts interpret it Jung believed that all wild animals in dreams indicate that our emotions have run riot in some way. The lion is the king of beasts, so the most appropriate response to this nightmare is to ask yourself which emotion is currently ruling you. A threatening lion suggests that you are experiencing a dominant emotion that you are not yet ready to face. If the lion is raging as he chases you, for example, you are running as hard as you can from overpowering feelings of anger. The lion can indicate that you feel swallowed up or consumed by these strong emotions.

The id, as defined by Freud (see page 12 of Dreams) is easily compared to a wild animal. A nightmare in which you are being chased by a lion would suggest that you want to run back to unconsciousness and to become oblivious to the wild emotions inherent in the lion symbol. Perhaps these strong emotions concern your father. As the ruler of the jungle, the lion is traditionally viewed as a father figure.

Try this to gain insight Because of its strength and ferocity, the lion can often symbolize the struggle between our mental and emotional realms. You may dream of a lion because you are controlling or are being controlled by someone else. Ask yourself, who it is you regard in your life as ruler of the kingdom? When you have spent time on that question, try associating your current waking life with these two sayings:
- pride comes before a fall
- throwing someone to the lions

Symbolizes pride, feeling territorial, issues with a father figure

Strength vs. stealth

In the wild, lions and hyenas are enemies, but they complement one another. The lion is magnificent, proud, and ruler of its territory, while the hyena is an opportunist and lives off the lion's kill. If you have a nightmare of both, ask yourself which was stronger. Each represents an instinct in our personal unconscious, and your nightmare will tell you which instinct is most prevalent at the moment. The dream's message may be telling you to stop taking the scraps in life and to become the king that you are.

The Vulture

Generally, we have negative associations with the vulture because it waits around hungrily for animals to die so that it can devour them. Its association with death is so strong that, in a nightmare, the vulture is often accompanied by characters who are dying or dead. More positively, it has been associated with mystical, even magical, abilities, one of which is being able to carry the souls of the dead in its body. Generally, however, the vulture is linked with pestilence, disease, and a rotten ending. If the vulture appears alongside a theme of war or battle, the implication is that the good side will be defeated. If you or someone close to you is ill, a vulture is not a favorable omen.

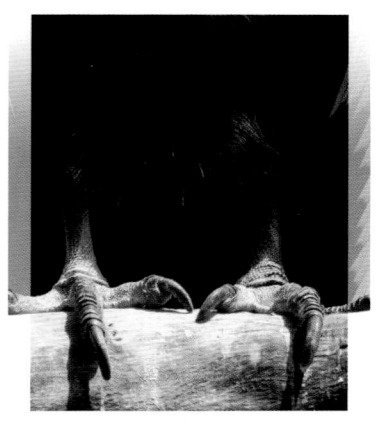

How dream analysts interpret it Wars often occur in the psyche as one part of it fights for dominance over another. This is especially true when the battle involves fledgling parts of the self that are yet to become fully formed. The fatalist in you, for example, may be doing battle with the budding opportunist. Just like the hyena, the vulture preys on the weak, so this nightmare can alert you to a part of yourself that needs protection. Look at what your vulture is consuming. Its carrion represents the part of you that needs to be uplifted or helped.

Freud, who linked the word "vulture" with "vulva," saw this as a dream about sex. A vulture carrying its prey up into the sky can be seen as a symbolic visualization of the passionate heights that sexual activity can reach. The Harpies of Greek mythology, who had the wings of vultures, feed into Freud's interpretation of female sexual energy gone awry. These unpleasant birdlike creatures use their cunning to beguile.

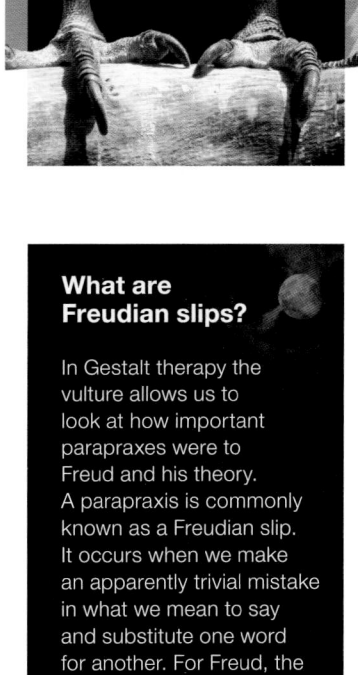

What are Freudian slips?

In Gestalt therapy the vulture allows us to look at how important parapraxes were to Freud and his theory. A parapraxis is commonly known as a Freudian slip. It occurs when we make an apparently trivial mistake in what we mean to say and substitute one word for another. For Freud, the mistake represents the breaking through of the unconscious. An apparent slip of the tongue actually represents our real feelings and beliefs.

Try this to gain insight You can use word association to work with this nightmare. The exercise below suggests eight levels of association. Write your responses down in your journal so that you can review them at the end of the exercise.

1. Say the first word that comes into your mind after "vulture."
2. Now do the same for the word you associated with vulture.
3. Repeat this six times.
4. What did you learn about yourself or someone else?

Symbolizes death, heaven, sexual power

The Snake

The snake is a common visitor to our nightmares. It has an ancient symbolic history, which accounts for the many cultural variations in its meaning. In Christian ideology it represents evil or temptation, whereas in Asian and Native American cultures, it represents wisdom, healing, and problem solving. In Western culture the snake is also associated with medicine, which has used the caduceus, a winged staff encircled by two snakes, as a motif since the seventh century. For children, a dream of snakes usually indicates anxiety. For adults, it may symbolize the penis, evil, or the poisonous spoken word.

How dream analysts interpret it Jung wrote extensively about the meaning of snakes. He believed that the snake was a symbol of transcendence, so a dream of one contains the positive message that you will overcome a problem. If you are bitten by a snake in a nightmare and recover, he saw this as a sign of increased maturity. This is because the snake's bite is often associated with temptation—the implication is that you have overcome temptation and achieved a higher state of awareness.

Freud also gave a lot of attention to this symbol. For him, the snake was a phallus. Research shows that snake dreams are most common during adolescence or puberty, which gives some weight to this interpretation. He also said that we should take note of the size and color of the snake in a dream, as well as its behavior. A large snake reflects the sexual feelings a child may have toward his or her father. As the child gets older, the snake will become smaller. A red snake will indicate intense emotion, whereas a green snake suggests emotional pain or jealousy.

Try this to gain insight This is an ideal dream symbol to incubate (see pages 30–31 of Dreams) because it encourages transcendence. If you have a recurring nightmare of snakes, try lucidity to explore its message. Follow the instructions for inducing lucidity on pages 32–33 of Dreams, and ask your snake:
1. What do you have to tell me?
2. Which of your abilities do I need to make me a better person?

Now make friends with the snake before letting it go.

Symbolizes transcendence, healing, initiation

What type of snake are you dreaming about?

A dream snake may be a mythical creature (see page 51). If you dream of a snake, look it up to see if it is linked to a myth. The snake is a powerful symbol and its appearance in your dream was probably significant. Did your snake have wings? If so, it was a serpent. The serpent's position will indicate the balance between good and evil in you, the dreamer, or in a current situation. If close to the ground, it is close to evil. The higher it is, the closer it is to heaven.

The Shark

There is something prehistoric about the shark. It has evolved very little over time and, as king of the sea, it has incredible survival strategies. It never sleeps. The shark's primary instincts are to kill and eat. Some shark species will follow the scent of blood over hundreds of miles to reach a food source. On arrival, it will engage in a feeding frenzy with any competing sharks in order to meet its sole need. This magnificent killer is a sleek, bone-chilling vision, both in real life and in our nightmares.

How dream analysts interpret it A shark may represent deep-rooted resentment, or even frenzied anger, which the dreamer is holding in his or her personal unconscious. In this sense the shark is present as a less evolved form of the shadow. If you have had a shark dream and this interpretation seems accurate, you will need to acknowledge some uncomfortable feelings that you have kept hidden. Rage is not socially acceptable in Western culture, even when it is a natural reaction to being poorly treated. If not anger, the shark in a dream or nightmare may signify fear. Do you sense danger in someone, or in your present surroundings? You don't need to watch a movie to imagine the terror of being circled by a shark.

Very often the most basic of human emotions is hidden in animal symbolism. A shark, of course, lives in the water. In Freudian theory, water is associated with emotion. So a dream of a shark may represent unacceptable, dangerous emotions that the dreamer would prefer to keep submerged in the unconscious.

Questions to ask yourself If a shark appears in your dreams, ask yourself the following questions:
1. When have you sensed danger recently?
2. Is there someone you know that reminds you of a shark?
3. Are you currently angry with someone or are you harboring a grudge?
4. With what or whom do you associate the word "predator?"

Symbolizes resentment, danger, very old hurts

What is the shark in your nightmares?

The shark never sleeps and never stops moving. It spends its life searching for food, which makes it an excellent predator. A dream shark may indicate an eating disorder or someone who is afraid of insomnia. As always, the meaning of a symbol will be particular to the dreamer and his or her associations. Someone who has studied sharks is less likely to dream of them in relation to intense fear. Although there are 360 species of sharks, only a very small proportion of these poses a threat to humans.

Being Murdered

This nightmare may not involve your actual murder, but it may focus on the events leading up to it. The dreamer often wakes up at the point of death. Being murdered is a very common nightmare theme. It is most likely to present itself when the dreamer is under stress or feeling threatened, as a symbolic playing out of the emotions that the person is experiencing. It is as though the dreamer is saying, "This situation, person, or feeling is killing me."

How dream analysts interpret it Jung, who looked on every part of a dream as an aspect of the dreamer, would say that an element of the dreamer's personality is threatening the rest of the psyche. This aspect may manifest itself in waking life as depression or anxiety.

How old were you in this dream? If you were younger than in your waking life, then according to Freud, the superego, or the older, more socialized aspect of your personality, may be punishing you for what it considers to be inappropriate behavior. If you were older in your dream than in waking life, you may be finding it hard to face your future. A woman in her thirties, for example, might visualize herself in a nightmare as an old hag being murdered. The old woman's murder signifies this dreamer's fear of aging.

Try this to gain insight If you are having this nightmare frequently, try the following exercise:

1. First think about who or what is trying to murder you. Then ask yourself, what is threatening you in life right now? Apply the question to your relationships (with yourself as well as other people), social life, family life, and work.
2. Now re-enter the dream. Use the first person and the present tense as you retell the story, but this time change the ending so that it gives you back control of the situation. Rather than finishing with your murder, try changing the attacker into a friend and start a conversation. Ask this person why he or she wants to kill you.

Symbolizes feeling threatened

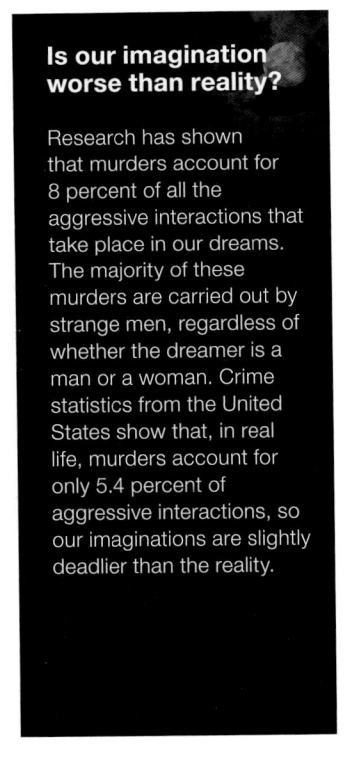

Is our imagination worse than reality?

Research has shown that murders account for 8 percent of all the aggressive interactions that take place in our dreams. The majority of these murders are carried out by strange men, regardless of whether the dreamer is a man or a woman. Crime statistics from the United States show that, in real life, murders account for only 5.4 percent of aggressive interactions, so our imaginations are slightly deadlier than the reality.

Being the Victim

The victim is a very powerful archetype, and it can be a tempting role to adopt in waking life. Because of its importance, engaging with this character during dream work can be an empowering experience. Once you have examined your habitual behavior and the victim's role in this, you are in a better position to realize your own power and take responsibility. Look through your nightmare journal to review how often you play this character. Now look at your waking life to find out whether there is a parallel. Is this your common response to people you find challenging?

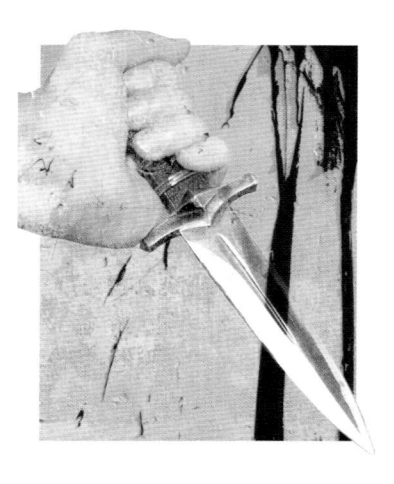

How dream analysts interpret it Jung defined an individuated person as someone who has reached his or her potential and is able to reflect honestly upon past behavior. This person, who Jung believed we should all aim to become, knows that if things go wrong in life, it is often because we've made a choice based upon instant gratification or avoiding fear, both of which often lead to negative consequences later. The victim is almost always to blame for these choices. He enters our nightmares when we feel we can do nothing to rescue ourselves. Sunk in self-pity, he is the part of us that feels at the mercy of whomever is victimizing us. If you have this nightmare, Jung would encourage you to see it as an opportunity. Reflect on how you were treated as the victim and how you would like to be treated. You can then set boundaries for yourself in your interactions with other people. If someone steps over a boundary by, for example, putting you down, you can turn the nightmare on its head and choose to stand up for yourself.

Questions to ask yourself Cut down on both nightmares and negative thinking by refusing to allow the victim to be a dominant force in waking life. Cognitive behavioral therapists say that we don't address behaviors that cause us distress because they have a payoff. In other words, acting as a victim can be a way of avoiding responsibility. Ask yourself the questions below. It is important to be truthful in your answers.

1. What are the benefits in my dream life of being a victim?
2. Where am I a victim in waking life?

Symbolizes how we expect to be treated, irresponsibility

Is there a gender tendency?

In every aggressive interaction there is an aggressor and a victim. A study conducted in 2008 by the Dream Research Group in the U.K. found that men more often dream that they are the aggressor, while women more often dream they are the victim. The stance of the dreamer also predicts how the dream is later perceived. When the dreamer is a victim, he or she is more likely to report the dream as a nightmare. If the dreamer is the aggressor, the dream is more likely to be remembered as pleasant.

Becoming Sick

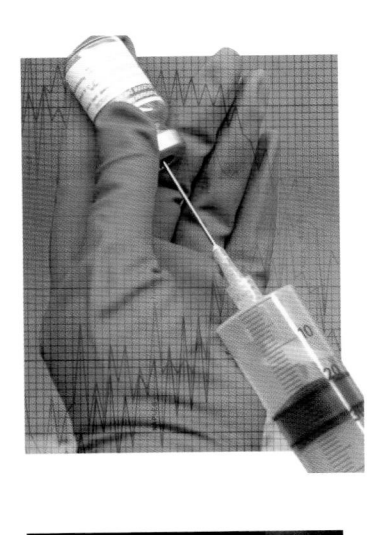

This is a very common nightmare. It is notorious for arousing the most intense emotions in the dreamer, who wakes up from the experience feeling very distressed. The illness varies, but it is the key to understanding the dream's meaning. Particular attention should be paid to the part of the body affected and the symptoms of the illness. In many cases, the illness represents emotional difficulties that the dreamer has yet to address. These difficulties usually involve vulnerability, either on the part of the dreamer or his or her perception of it in someone else.

How dream analysts interpret it Dreams of illness often represent the various elements that make up a complex (see also page 68 of Dreams). Jung said that if we don't deal with our emotional concerns, we suffer for it in the long run. If becoming sick is one of your nightmares, one of your complexes is probably taking over and needs to be analyzed while you are awake. The story of your dream will help you identify the source of the complex. If you dream you have a brain tumor and are worried about how you will tell everyone, this suggests some difficulty in communication with people close to you.

Try this to gain insight Dreams of sickness may symbolize different things. The list below will help you explore the links between your illness and the emotional problem it represents.

1. The head—a problem here relates to clarity of thinking or having too much going on in your head.
2. The mouth—this suggests that there is something you want to say but haven't been able to.
3. The breasts—this area relates to nourishment, actual or emotional, and sexuality.
4. The stomach—if the illness is here, ask yourself whether you are finding something hard to digest.
5. The heart—there are numerous metaphors for the heart, but start by asking yourself if your heart is broken.
6. The legs—if immobility is the problem in your nightmare, ask yourself where in your life you feel stuck.

Symbolizes vulnerability, unprocessed emotional concerns, the appearance of complexes

Which parts of the body occur most in nightmares?

Researchers have counted references to body parts in many dream reports. The parts of the body most often referred to are the hands and feet, although it is not known why this is. A body part is often mentioned in the context of a nightmare focusing on illness. Men report the illness of the dreamer or other dream characters in 21 percent of dreams and women in 25 percent of dreams. If we dream of someone who is seriously ill, it is usually someone very close to us in our waking lives.

Losing Something Precious

There are many versions of this dream as there are precious things. You might misplace keys, a wallet, your house, a pet, or perhaps your children. These nightmares represent our emotional attachment to people, places, and objects. Rather than the search, the focus of the nightmare is often the feelings we are left with once we realize that what we held so dear is no longer in our possession. As our panic grows, we go through disbelief, shock, and denial. The absence of our precious thing often prevents us from continuing whatever we were doing in the nightmare, which effectively stalls its story line.

How dream analysts interpret it Jung recognized that we all proceed through various life changes and major life events. There's no avoiding these important transitions, and as we try hard to adapt to them, our dream recall increases. A dream of losing something precious reflects the desire for things to stay the way they were. The search we go on and our accompanying feelings of disbelief reflect the reluctance we have to change and take the next step of our journey toward individuation. Change is undeniably difficult, but working with this nightmare and making conscious our fears can do a great deal to help us adapt.

Freud believed that purses, wallets, and some articles of clothing, including hats, in dreams represent the vagina. So if you lose a purse in a nightmare, one interpretation would be that you have lost your virginity, or sexual naivete, or something precious relating to your sexual identity.

Questions to ask yourself Jung believed that losing something in a dream reflects a loss we perceive in our waking life. If you have this nightmare, ask yourself:

1. Which loss in my waking life am I trying to accept (or deny)?

2. Am I at the beginning of a major life transition?

Symbolizes life transitions, acceptance, loss of persona

Is what we lose significant?

If you lose an item of clothing or a personal item, such as jewelry, your nightmare may be hinting at a chink in your persona. The loss of this type of object usually relates to the way we clothe our waking selves to be regarded as socially acceptable. You might lose a purse or briefcase in a dream, for example, if you sense that your personal identity is threatened. If, however, you lose a person, particularly a child, you are having a classic anxiety dream.

Being Alone & Isolated

In some dreams we are utterly alone. You may not even recognize your environment, which increases your sense of isolation.

When people report this nightmare, they often use a word that describes their most painful feelings: abandonment. Being alone and isolated is one of the most profound nightmares a dreamer can experience. It also holds valuable existential promise. In some cultures, isolation often precedes great spiritual insight. This experience may be engineered during waking life through rites of passage, such as when young males are sent hunting alone for the first time. The isolation they must endure marks their transition from boy to manhood.

How dream analysts interpret it At the core of every psyche is a person's authentic self. The self is surrounded by the noise and busyness of the persona but, as we grow and develop, our self grows more pronounced. We become more confident about showing this true self, rather than our persona, to the world. This dream may be unpleasant, but going into a metaphorical wilderness represents a great step forward spiritually. Jung would say that the dream is preparing you to be alone and face your shadow, or the negative aspects of your character, so that you may accept them and reunite as a complete, balanced person. How much of a people person are you? We all need to belong to some extent. Some people fear being alone more than anything, so they stay in unsatisfactory relationships rather than face their fear. In these cases the nightmare plays out feelings that the dreamer has a habit of repressing. Until the feelings are acknowledged and worked through, the dreamer is emotionally trapped. For others, this dream puts them in touch with the part of them that is a natural loner.

Questions to ask yourself There can be a significant difference between feeling alone and feeling abandoned, although both feelings may be manifested as a nightmare. Explore the meaning of your dream by asking the following:

1. Did I feel alone and isolated? Would I gain from time alone?
2. Did I feel abandoned? Do I feel abandoned by someone in real life? Do I need to connect more with those around me?

Symbolizes spiritual growth, repressed feelings, grief

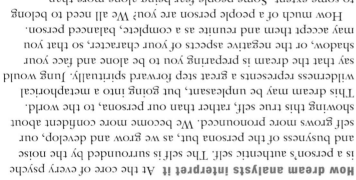

How does being alone manifest itself in your nightmare?

Nightmares of this type are common when we feel vulnerable, for example, when a relationship ends. Being alone can present itself in various ways. A dream in which you are traveling alone in a foreign landscape can be very positive, indicating that you are going to parts of the self that have never been visited. But, if you find yourself quarantined in a nightmare, ask which part of you feels so unclean that you have to keep it separate from others.

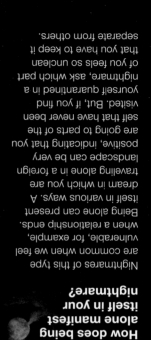

Being Unable to Move

This classic nightmare has been experienced and reported across cultures and throughout history. Typically, another scenario plays out first, which ends with the dreamer feeling immobilized, often as part of what scientists call a sleep paralysis event (see page 24). If you have this dream, you won't have to dig deep to uncover its meaning. While many of the dreams and nightmares covered in this book require lengthy decoding, this one can be approached as a straightforward metaphor. It means that we feel stuck or unable to proceed in some area of our lives.

How dream analysts interpret it Jung's approach to understanding nightmares (and dreams) comes under the broad heading of psychodynamic psychology, which describes the idea that the psyche is always changing and that it has an energy of its own. When exploring this dream, it's also appropriate to remember Jung's mantra that every aspect of a dream represents part of the dreamer. A dream in which you cannot move, therefore, indicates that you have accessed an area of your unconscious mind that you are stuck in and need to take action to get moving again. You might, for example, have a nightmare in which you are stuck in an elevator at work. This would suggest that your rise to a higher floor, or an attempt to reach the top in the workplace is being stalled somehow. You would need to do something in waking life to get the elevator moving once more.

Questions to ask yourself Nightmares in which you are unable to move are often accompanied by a need to escape from something or someone. Ask yourself which of the following archetypes you are running from:
1. The shadow? Do you find it hard to admit to the darker aspects of your personality?
2. The victim? Are you putting up with a bad situation and blaming other people for it?
3. The addict? Do you seek instant gratification in your approach to life rather than delayed satisfaction? Your answer will show you what you need to face before you can move on.

Symbolizes being stuck, stagnation

What am I running from?

When dream researchers Calvin Hall and Robert Van de Castle examined dream content in 1966, being stuck or unable to move was counted as a misfortune. This type of misfortune is very common in nightmares and is central to most sleep paralysis events. A common example is when the dreamer tries to run from something frightening but discovers that his or her legs won't work. The appropriate questions to ask here would be what exactly the dreamer is running from, and why it is so difficult to move forward.

Being Naked in Public

Dreams of being naked in public are characterized by feelings of intense shame and embarrassment. Not only are you naked but also you have no means of covering yourself up and escaping everyone else's stares. The exposure is often made all the worse by the fact that you have come out into the open from an enclosed space. As much as you wish the earth would swallow you up, it doesn't. Very occasionally, the dreamer uses this nightmarish opportunity to throw off the chains and to feel free and unencumbered, but this most positive of outcomes is rare. Most of us go on squirming until the end.

How dream analysts interpret it Jung said this dream was about the persona (see also page 40 of Dreams). Your persona is the version of yourself you show the world. When you sense the mask is slipping or you lose your clothes in a nightmare, you stand alone and uncomfortable. For some people, the equivalent might be showing themselves without makeup or a wig for the first time. There are many types of masks, some more literal than others, and we piece them together as we emerge out of early childhood. In a positive sense, dreams like this may come when people try to get to know themselves better and suspect that what they are finding is not enough.

Alternatively, a dream of being naked can reflect a situation in which the dreamer feels overexposed. You may have started a new venture, for example, or be getting to know a new group of people. The persona hides everything that we don't like about ourselves. The thought of revealing our shadow self generates the anxiety that causes the nightmare.

Questions to ask yourself It is often more useful to focus on the emotions you experienced during a nightmare rather than the specific story line. Ask yourself the following questions to discover the origin of your feelings of shame and embarrassment:

1. Where did the dream take place?
2. Who was watching or who saw me naked?
3. What is it about the people staring at me that makes me want to impress them?
4. How do I fall short of this aim to impress in waking life?

Symbolizes lack of protection, exposure

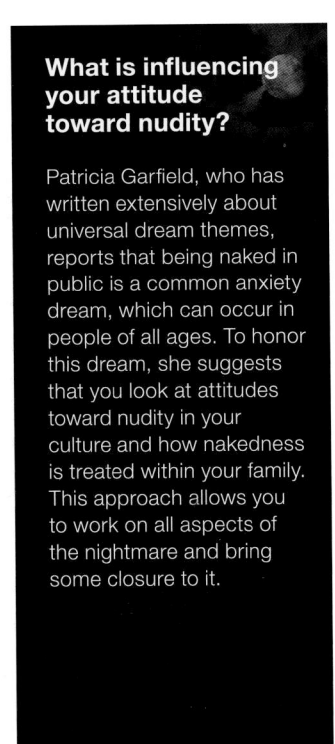

What is influencing your attitude toward nudity?

Patricia Garfield, who has written extensively about universal dream themes, reports that being naked in public is a common anxiety dream, which can occur in people of all ages. To honor this dream, she suggests that you look at attitudes toward nudity in your culture and how nakedness is treated within your family. This approach allows you to work on all aspects of the nightmare and bring some closure to it.

Technology Breaking Down

Technology in dreams is on the rise. A hundred years ago the equivalent anxiety manifested itself in nightmares about writing letters and looking at photographs. The dreamer might have been tasked with writing to everyone in the world, or been forced to look at photographs of mangled bodies. Nowadays these older forms of communication have morphed into broken computers, cellphones that don't work, or trains that go off the rails. A breakdown in communication is normally the root cause. Alternatively, this nightmare may signify some kind of block that is preventing you from reaching a goal.

How dream analysts interpret it The various components of the psyche do not exist in isolation, and they communicate with each other principally through dreams. A common version of this nightmare involves the dreamer in a dangerous situation and in need of assistance. The dreamer picks up the phone to call for help and cannot get through. Jung would say that this reflects one aspect of the self calling on another. Because the psyche deals in archetypes, the dreamer is calling on either the rescuer or the hero to come and save the day but is unable to find the personal resource to meet the challenge.

It's useful to approach this dream by identifying exactly what isn't working and applying that to an aspect of your psyche. You might dream of a laptop breaking down, for example. A computer is made up of many different parts, each of which has a different job. If your laptop runs out of memory, you could benefit from shedding old ways of thinking to free up space.

Questions to ask yourself If we go along with Jung's thinking that cellphones and computers are about communication, then nightmares of this nature suggest a communication breakdown. To discover the nature of the breakdown in your case, ask yourself the following:

1. Whom was I trying to call?
2. What does this person or service represent to me?
3. What do I want to say to them that I haven't already?

Symbolizes communication breakdown, not being able to get through, prodromal warnings (dreams that foretell physiological health or illness)

What does the breakdown symbolize?

This type of nightmare can be linked to the prodromal nature of dreaming (dreams that foretell physiological health or illness, see page 79 of Dreams). A machine that fails to work may symbolize a part of the body that is breaking down or becoming ill. Blocked pipes may signify heart problems, whereas a computer can suggest your brain is overloaded or out of memory, and vehicles such as cars or boats, that won't start may represent the body in general.

Falling

Have you ever dreamed you were falling from the top of a high building or out of a plane without a parachute? Maybe you were closer to Earth and fell headlong into a bottomless pit. Falling is a dream theme that has been reported throughout history and across cultures. The act of falling has many variations and may occur in any number of situations. All the factors need to be taken into account when interpreting the dream's meaning. In general falling can be viewed as a metaphor for helplessness.

How dream analysts interpret it Falling commonly relates to the dreamer's spiritual, religious, or moral values. If you fall from a high place, the implication is that you have failed in some way to live up to these personal standards. If the fall is long, it may be that you set yourself up to fall by expecting too much of yourself and having set an unrealistic expectation. In the process of aiming very high, you cannot help but build in a fear of falling. Falling may also symbolize a fall from grace or a fall in social standing. It is always appropriate to ask, when working with a falling dream, where in waking life you feel less than or lower than those around you.

Questions to ask yourself When you consider what a dream of this nature means, reflect on the whole experience. Some of the questions you might ask yourself include:

1. Where in my life do I feel helpless?
2. Am I facing change in the near future?
3. Do I feel on the brink of danger in some way?
4. Have I done something recently that I feel bad about?
5. Have I lost status socially?
6. Has a relationship or project fallen through? If another dream character was involved, it usually means that you feel unsupported by that person. This other character may have pushed you and caused your fall. In other versions of the nightmare, you might fall alongside archetypal characters, which suggests that they are losing their dominance in your psyche. Falling with a dark, evil figure would indicate that your shadow self is releasing its hold on you.

Symbolizes falling in either social or moral standing, natural fears, feeling unsupported

What happens if you hit the ground?

A dream about falling can end in different ways. A soft landing is a good outcome, signifying that the dreamer has the necessary cushioning within his or her personal armory to break the fall. A hard landing or no landing at all suggests the dreamer is still in free fall. A shock landing suggests the dreamer's unconscious mind is trying to shock the dreamer into awareness. If you have a shock landing, pay attention to your first thoughts on waking. They usually hint at what your unpleasant dream is trying to tell you.

Teeth Falling Out

Almost everyone has a bad dental dream at some point. Typically, the dreamer looks in the mirror and suddenly notices teeth that are loose and falling out. Sometimes the dreamer will deal with the problem by pulling the teeth out, which doesn't hurt but is terribly distressing. As in real life, losing teeth is a deeply personal matter, which has a negative impact on self-image. Nightmares on this theme almost always concern identity.

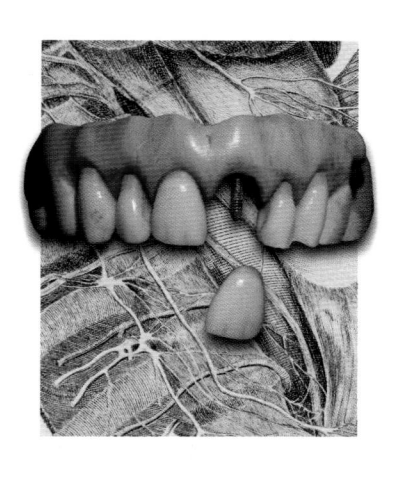

How dream analysts interpret it Jung believed these dreams relate to aging. A teeth dream may be conveying a message from your unconscious that, like everyone else, you are getting older and losing your more youthful appearance. You may even, in actuality, be losing your teeth. Although you will have acknowledged this process unconsciously, your nightmare is insisting that your waking, conscious self take notice. This dream may also represent a loss of identity or the fear of this. A nightmare of rotten or infected teeth suggests you are festering with anger or feeling overtaken by social conformity and the restrictions it places on you.

Freud told his male patients who had this dream that it represented their fear of castration or the loss of their masculine power. He told women that it was a wish for motherhood. A tooth, like a baby, is small, and its removal is bloody.

Questions to ask yourself Dreams about the mouth can represent unspoken feelings. If your nightmare contained teeth falling out or any restriction of your mouth, explore it by asking the following:

1. How did I feel in this dream?
2. Do I find it difficult to express anger, disappointment, or any other socially difficult feeling?
3. If my teeth were feelings, which ones would they be?
4. Whom would I like to say these things to?

Symbolizes losing face, identity, broodiness

Have I "lost face"?

Dr. Gayle Delaney of the Delaney & Flowers Dream Center in San Francisco disagrees with both Jung's and Freud's interpretations of teeth dreams. She writes that, in her experience as a dream therapist, loss of teeth usually means the dreamer feels he or she has "lost face" in some area or looks bad to someone else. This is especially likely if the loss of teeth is accompanied by feelings of embarrassment or humiliation.

The Labyrinth

The labyrinth is one of the oldest geometrical designs. It is usually complex and either square or circular. Finding the entrance to a dream labyrinth may be easy, but once inside, the dreamer is confronted with one of two challenging journeys. Either the labyrinth has a continuous path that takes the dreamer to its core, or it is a maze, with twists, turns, and dead ends, which make finding the center or the exit a puzzle. The most significant manifestation of the labyrinth in a nightmare is one that takes the dreamer downward. The descent represents confusion, puzzlement, and a lowering into the unconscious.

How dream analysts interpret it Whereas the mandala is the symbol for the self (see page 47 of Dreams), the labyrinth is the symbol for life in its totality. Jung believed that this was one of the most important of all the dream symbols. It represents transformation. The journey through the labyrinth can be compared to the journey through life. It is full of dead ends, intersections, and false starts. When, or if, the dreamer reaches the center, he or she has found the holy grail: the meaning of life. At this point you have explored yourself fully and are whole.

Doesn't sound much like a nightmare? It isn't if you find your way through the labyrinth successfully. In a nightmare of the labyrinth, you are lost, afraid, and unsure about which way to go next. This is indicative of how you feel about life. This nightmare is a symbolic journey into the unconscious. Along its dark tunnels you brush up against all the murky, frightening and, crucially, as yet unknown aspects of your psyche.

Try this to gain insight Like the mandala, the labyrinth is a useful symbol to re-create as part of your dream work. Try drawing a labyrinth like the one above that fits the shape of your own life. It needs to feel right for you. Alternatively, you could write your lifeline. Begin with your birth and include all the major events in your life to the present day. Do not focus on the bad things that have happened, but include the positive, too. This exercise will help to give you a balanced perspective of your life's journey, with all its highs and lows.

Symbolizes feeling lost or confused

Can the labyrinth symbolize other trials?

This is an extract from a dream report: "I dreamed I was in a labyrinth and that I couldn't find my way to the center. I could see over the top of the walls and realized I was being chased by demons. I had to get to the middle since it was the only place I would be safe. I woke up feeling very scared and like the nightmare was really important." The dreamer was diagnosed with breast cancer two months after having this dream. The labyrinth represented the anatomy of her breast.

Buildings

The environment of a nightmare often contains buildings. These constructions are usually dark, foreboding, and dominate the landscape. Dream researchers have found that buildings add to the darkness of a dream's mood and content. Typically, the dreamer decides to go into one of the buildings, and the next stage of nightmare follows. The building may be a symbol of the self, and entering it heralds an exploration of the unconscious.

How dream analysts interpret it We project our current self-image onto buildings in dreams, and your dream buildings will reflect the state of your psychological and physical well-being. Jung once dreamed of a golden castle, and this encouraged him to take his ideas into the world as a teacher. He was the elaborate castle, and the smaller surrounding buildings represented others in his circle. Similarly, exploring buildings in nightmares can lead to important discoveries that will affect your waking behavior.

Freud liked to examine dream buildings for their phallic potential, which denotes male energy and power. He wanted to know whether the building had monuments outside or columns forming part of its structure. He may have asked if the doors were open, because this would indicate sexual possibilities. Doors kept firmly shut would suggest an inhospitable sexual tension between the dreamer and whoever was on the dreamer's mind.

Questions to ask yourself To understand the meaning of buildings, first establish some features. Use this checklist:

1. Were the buildings old or new? Their age represents the age of the issue being presented in the nightmare.
2. Were they single-story or high-rise buildings? High-rise buildings represent thoughts and single-story buildings represent feelings and instincts.
3. Were they in good shape or damaged? Am I wounded or in need of essential repair?
4. Could I find my way or was this difficult? Am I dealing with this problem or am I finding it difficult to find a route out?
5. Were the buildings like a castle or more humble? Is my ego large (a castle) or do I need to think more of myself?

Symbolizes current perception of the self, the state of our psychological and physical health

Is this a fear of the unknown?

In his book *The Wilderness of Dreams*, Kelly Bulkeley approaches the world of dreams as underexplored terrain. When we are in this terrain during nightmares, and when we reflect on them, we fear what we don't understand. Nightmares may take us to barren landscapes or crowded cities, and we cut a small figure within them. Bulkeley writes that by paying this world of the unknown more attention, we can realize our waking concerns and use this knowledge to do something about them.

Travel

Nightmares often include travel, especially the nightmares reported by men. You might choose anything to travel by: a car, airplane, train, boat, elevator, bike, or perhaps even a bird or laser beam. All modes of transport do the same thing, which is to move you from one point to another. It may sound obvious, but in a nightmare this movement suggests that you are not happy with your current waking situation. The type of transport you choose can provide clues to the reason for the discontentment.

How dream analysts interpret it Jung wrote that transport in dreams reflects the way we are functioning psychologically. So, for example, a stalled car can mean that you feel unable to move forward with a current problem. If the car is careening out of control and you are trying desperately to apply the brakes, you sense your life is moving too fast, perhaps in the wrong direction. The vehicle may also describe the way a dreamer perceives his or her physical body. A Corvette is sexy and slim, whereas a van is more pragmatic. Associated with this is the idea that if someone else is in control of the vehicle in your nightmare, you do not see yourself as being in charge of your own life.

Most vehicles in Freudian dream interpretation are viewed as symbols for the genitals. Freud believed that dreams about travel are usually about sex. A boat may dock, a car may park, and an airplane may land. In a nightmare, however, your travel (sexual) experience won't be either as smooth or successful.

Try this to gain insight To explore what your nightmare of travel means, start by focusing on the vehicle and its associations. The short list below should help start you off.

1. Cars—the body, or the physical self. If the car in your dream didn't start, ask yourself whether you need a checkup.
2. Boats—your state in relation to your emotional life. How was the voyage? A stormy passage can indicate emotional instability.
3. Airplanes—seeing yourself as above others. Did you crash? Did your inflated sense of self lead to your downfall?

Symbolizes the flow of psychological life, the need to move forward, how the dreamer perceives him or herself

Is travel a male nightmare?

Recent research in the U.K. comparing men's and women's nightmares has identified travel as one of the main themes of men's nightmares. The male dreamer may be driving a car that crashes, killing a close male friend who is with him. In other travel nightmares the male dreamer sees an airplane crashing so everyone on board, including his family, is killed. Both these examples involve dangers to people close to the dreamer, suggesting that men will choose a travel theme to express fears about significant others.

Tidal Waves

You are standing on a beach, looking out to sea. The water pulls back to the horizon and then, as you realize with horror that it's too late to get out of the way, it rushes back toward you as a massive tidal wave. The tidal wave is a universal nightmare. The dreamer often wakes up before the water hits or is engulfed by the waves and must struggle to survive. It is one of Jung's big dreams (see pages 14–15 of Dreams). The memory of this dramatic dream can last a lifetime.

How dream analysts interpret it For Jung, a dream of water was a manifestation of the unconscious. A tidal wave suggests that the dreamer feels overwhelmed by the contents of his or her unconscious and may not be ready to find out what it contains. The emotions contained in the wave will inevitably be unpleasant ones, which we have done our best to suppress while awake. This nightmare may also have an even deeper metaphorical meaning. As recent years have seen the catastrophic consequences of rogue waves around the world, the symbolism of tidal waves is currently very active. We know that these real-life tidal waves destroy without mercy. If this understanding of the tidal waves effect is applied to the psyche, a tidal wave dream not only suggests that your mind is overwhelmed but also that it is being swept clean. Water is a symbol of emotion, so the fresh start is an opportunity to begin honoring your feelings rather than hiding them away in your nightmares.

Can a tidal wave represent emotion?

Professor Ernest Hartmann explores tidal wave dreams in his book *Dreams & Nightmares: The Origin and Meaning of Dreams*. He suggests that the image is the visual representation of an emotion. For Hartmann, a tidal wave represents fear or terror. We can elaborate on this by saying that the tidal wave also represents being overwhelmed by these emotions.

Try this to gain insight Tidal wave nightmares lend themselves to rescripting or imagery rehearsal techniques (see pages 30–33) because they often recur. Try the following:
1. Write down the nightmare in your journal.
2. Next to it rewrite the ending in a way that suits you. For example, some people use big waves for sport. You could write that as the tidal wave approaches, you get out your surfboard and ride the wave. State explicitly that you no longer feel fear or terror. Put it on record that your achievement has filled you with exhilaration and awe.

Symbolizes feeling overwhelmed by emotion, trauma, emotional housekeeping

Fire

A nightmare that involves fire, a volcano, or a firestorm is very significant. The presence of fire is normally interpreted as energy that is both destructive and out of control. Whereas water in tidal waves suggests emotion generally, fire is a more specific dream symbol, representing anger. This nightmare is extraordinarily useful as it allows you to vent deep-seated, potentially destructive rage. A fire will purge the landscape of your dreams and enable you to rebuild. If you are a lucid dreamer, you may want to try containing the fire and revisualizing it as a nimbus or radiant light.

How dream analysts interpret it Jung liked to look on the bright side of any dreaming experience. The fire raging in your nightmare may be destroying those parts of your psyche that are no longer necessary, destructive, or diseased. If you find a closet of clothes on fire, for example, the suggestion is that you have less need of an outward persona because you are moving closer to your true self. If the fire is associated with a volcano, it indicates an eruption of psychic energy. In this case the dreamer should consider where the eruption is taking place. If you are on vacation abroad, for example, the source of the anger lies in your social life. It is also useful to establish whether your dream fire was natural or if it was started by someone else. In other words, is this your anger or someone else's?

Freud loved to play on words and encouraged his patients to do the same. If you have this nightmare, ask yourself if you are playing with fire or are getting your fingers burned in some area of your life. Like Jung, Freud also linked fire with sexual energy (libido) and death energy (Thanatos). Fire in a dream allows these energies to burn without anyone getting hurt in real life.

Questions to ask yourself If your nightmares often involve fires, ask yourself:
1. If the fire was a feeling, what feeling would it be?
2. If the fire was a situation, what situation would it be?
3. Who in my life at the moment do I consider to be hot in a sexual sense?

Symbolizes destructive forces, all-consuming energy, purification

Is experiencing a disaster better than imagining it?

In *Trauma and Dreams* (1996), Dr. Alana Seigel reports on a study of survivors of the firestorms in California in 1991. Two years afterward, people evacuated from their homes were more distressed than those who stayed and survived. The evacuees' dreams reflected death, injury, disaster, and out-of-control events. The findings suggest that their guilt at leaving the scene left them more psychologically damaged than the survivors who stayed and experienced the events firsthand.

Significant Others Are Sick

Every now and then an important dream character gets sick. In nightmares it is usually someone close to us in our waking life. The temptation when interpreting such a dream is to fast-forward to the death of the character and ignore the illness. However, it's the process of the illness that is central to understanding this dream, coupled with an appreciation that life changes tend to unfold over time and not as a result of single, isolated events. All types of illnesses may be presented in this nightmare, ranging from chronic conditions, such as arthritis, to sudden acute conditions, such as strokes, fevers, or cancers, that will befall the dream character as part of the dream's plot.

How dream analysts interpret it Illness in a dream is rarely what it seems. It usually reflects the dreamer's ability to perceive dysfunction and manifest it as dream imagery. Intuitively, we may sense a problem, either in ourselves or someone we know, before we become consciously aware of it. The key question to ask yourself in response to this nightmare is whether you or someone close to you currently has a disease, in either a physical, psychological, or emotional respect. You can then reflect on the nature of the illness in the nightmare to understand the cause of that disease in waking life.

Not many people know that Carl Jung was instrumental in developing the 12-step program that is used by Alcoholics Anonymous, Narcotics Anonymous, and other groups, such as Alanon, that support the families of people with an addictive behavior. People who are associated with addictive behaviors are especially likely to dream of sickness. The illness represents the disease experienced by the addict.

Questions to ask yourself If you dream of illness, ask:
1. Who is sick?
2. What is this nightmare trying to tell me so urgently?
3. Do I feel overresponsible in any area of my life? Do I feel burdened by my responsibility for someone?
4. If I changed the ending, how could the illness be cured? If possible, act on your answer to this question in waking life.

Symbolizes overresponsibility, addictive behavior, disease

What do body parts represent in nightmares?

Louise Hay, a therapist who worked with the dying, attributed psychological meaning to different parts of the body. Her approach may be useful in deciphering your nightmares. Here are three examples:

- The head—destructive thinking patterns.

- The hands—holding on too tight and needing to let go.

- Being overweight— a need for protection, or a barrier between the dreamer and the world.

The Appearance of Strangers

Do you dream mostly of people you know or of people you've never met? In general half of the characters in our nightmares are people we don't know in waking life. When pressed, dreamers usually say these strangers were male. You are more likely to invite strangers into your dreams, male or female, if you are depressed or suffering some other mental distress. Nothing helps a nightmare about isolation and loneliness so much as the certainty that you know no one. If you're an extrovert in real life, research suggests that you will welcome strangers more easily to your dreams than someone more introverted. Who was that? Did you know him? Strangers may also bring a certain mystery...

How dream analysts interpret it The focus throughout this book is on interpretations that promote psychological health and development. This is the basis of Carl Jung's approach. Jung believed that strangers in dreams are parts of the self that we are yet to become acquainted with and that have previously resided in the unconscious. Like Freud, he knew that the strangers may be frightening and can at first appear threatening. Nevertheless, he taught that they come into dreams intentionally to help the dreamer become a more complete person.

Another way to interpret this is to apply two of Freud's defense mechanisms. A stranger dream may be the result of projection: Your mind creates a stranger to carry the attributes you prefer not to claim as your own. Or the dream may involve an act of displacement: You dislike or attack a stranger in order to be rid of the aggressive feelings you have toward someone in waking life. Just as you might yell at the cat instead of a partner, you choose to vent your anger on a stranger because it is easier than addressing the person who has really made you angry.

Questions to ask yourself Strangers usually indicate aggression that is not acknowledged. Ask yourself the following:

1. Whom does this stranger remind me of?
2. Why am I angry with this stranger in the dream?
3. Why is this stranger angry or threatening me?
4. Does this relate to a waking situation or past event?

Symbolizes mysterious parts of the self, projected or displaced anger

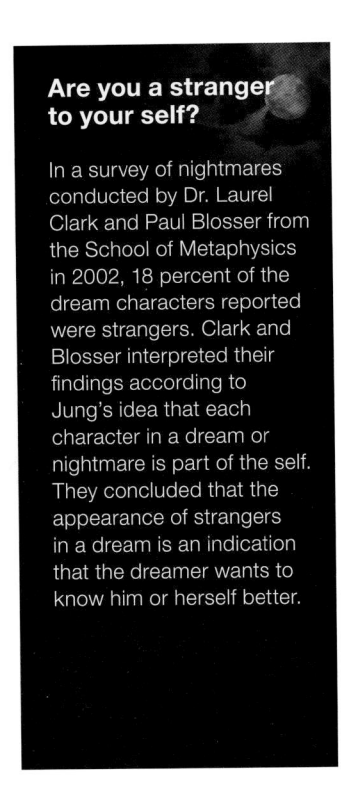

Are you a stranger to your self?

In a survey of nightmares conducted by Dr. Laurel Clark and Paul Blosser from the School of Metaphysics in 2002, 18 percent of the dream characters reported were strangers. Clark and Blosser interpreted their findings according to Jung's idea that each character in a dream or nightmare is part of the self. They concluded that the appearance of strangers in a dream is an indication that the dreamer wants to know him or herself better.

Death

There are two things we all know for certain. First, that we will die and, second, that we will lose others whom we love. Dreaming of someone dying rarely means that person is about to die in real life. These dreams usually indicate closure or a need for it. A death could also be read as a warning that if you don't take action, a relationship will soon fall apart.

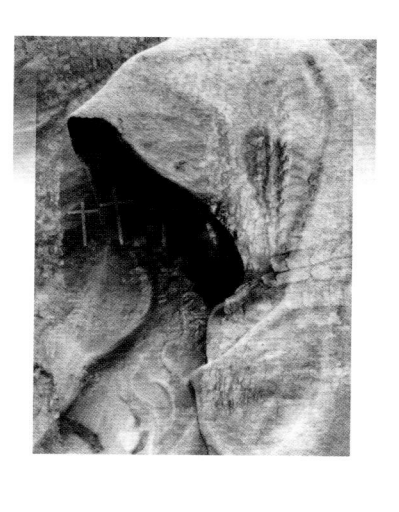

How dream analysts interpret it Jung believed that death, in the metaphorical sense, is needed over and over again in a lifetime and that every character in our dreams represents a part of ourselves. Dying allows us to be reborn or to be open to new aspects of ourselves. If you have this nightmare, you need to establish which part of yourself the dying person represents.

You can interpret this dream more literally if someone you know has died recently. Grief dreams may continue for two to ten years after a death. They go through stages, beginning with ones in which the dreamer reruns the death itself.

Understanding grief through nightmares Try to view these dreams positively. They can help you to:

1. Accept the reality—nightmares can replay feelings and events. "Dying again" dreams represent the first grief stage.
2. Work through the pain—nightmares in which intense sadness is felt can occur in the second phase of grief.
3. Adjust to life without that person—in the third phase of grief, the dreams often stop, or they may show the deceased as damaged or alongside symbols of death.
4. Come to peace—if dreams go to a fourth stage, the dreamer may see the deceased as young or well again. Best of all, the deceased gives a present to the dreamer before taking leave. By the fifth stage, the grief dreams will stop. The bereaved person has fond memories, but no longer feels that life is impossible without the deceased. If the grieving process goes wrong, it will take longer to reach this point. Toxic grief is the term used for grief that is stuck or unresolved. It may manifest itself as nightmares in which the deceased, wanting company, extends an invitation to the dreamer. In these cases special help or counseling should be sought.

Symbolizes loss, grief, stages of acceptance

Can nightmares help you move on?

This dream occurred five years after the dreamer's father had suddenly died, after nightmares in which she tried and failed to find him. *"I was at the airport and my father appeared at the other side of the barrier. He was boarding an airplane. He was wearing a Hawaiian shirt, brightly colored shorts, and he looked fantastic. He waved and said, 'Tell your Mom I'm fine. Don't worry, I'm doing just great.'"* The dreamer knew her nightmares about not saying good-bye were over. She had accepted her loss.

The End of the World

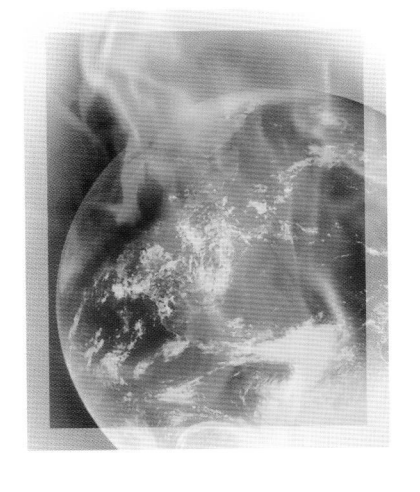

This category covers apocalyptic events, such as nuclear war, earthquakes, the planet being ravaged, or the human race dying out. For many, an end-of-the-world nightmare is one of the most significant dreams we ever have. Its impact can be so great that we remember it years later. It may include the deaths of the dreamer's family, which the dreamer can do nothing to prevent. The dreamer wakes with a sense of dread and foreboding. These nightmares usually occur in early adulthood and mark the end of childhood. The dream should not be taken literally, but as an indication that life as the dreamer knows it is coming to an end.

How dream analysts interpret it With all versions of this nightmare, the dreamer faces the world, or what remains of it, after a devastating event. If the nightmare does not reflect a literal fear of apocalypse, the dreamer needs to establish what has happened to "end the world" in waking life. Often, the nightmare occurs when the dreamer has been traumatized, perhaps after a car accident or house fire. But the event does not have to be as traumatic as this. An ordinary event, such as moving, also has the potential to alter the dreamer's perception of the world and who he or she is within it.

Questions to ask yourself This type of dream can show that something important has happened to the dreamer on a personal level, and it can recur unless the cause is addressed. Ask yourself:
1. Did the world end because of an environmental catastrophe? A natural end suggests that the trauma is a natural life event, such as the death of someone close.
2. Was the cause man-made? A nuclear explosion or chemical warfare might suggest that the cause is unrelated to natural life events. It may be an huge mortgage or bankruptcy.
3. Was the world invaded by aliens? Has someone or something come into my life that is unknown and threatens everything I care for?

Symbolizes survival of the planet, balance in the psyche, loss of control

Does the fate of the world rest with you?

People sometimes have nightmares in which everyone in the world is going to die. Typically, the dreamer is the only one who realizes the danger because the cause of death is very cleverly hidden or the object of destruction appears innocuous. Reports of these dreams describe the release of poisonous gases, large balls exploding, and, in recent years, the whole world being infected with AIDS. These dream events suggest the dreamer feels responsible for things that are, in fact, beyond his or her control.

Attending a Funeral

In real life a funeral is a carefully orchestrated event, designed as an official good-bye to someone who has died. Our nightmares allow far greater flexibility. A funeral in your dreams may, for example, begin as a wedding. But regardless of the dream's permutations, a funeral always signifies an end. The dreamer is saying good-bye to someone or something that he or she unconsciously feels is dead. This is why a nightmare that includes a funeral is so upsetting. The dreamer, until the point of the nightmare, may not have been aware of being ready to let go.

How dream analysts interpret it Carl Jung's last recalled dream was of a great stone, similar to a headstone. Written upon it were the words, "And this shall be a sign unto you of Wholeness and Oneness." He took this as an indication that his life's work was done and died a few days later. Jung believed that funeral dreams were great events. He explained that their finality allows us to redeem ourselves. After a funeral dream, having said good-bye to a person, a part of our psyche, or a way of behaving, we have a chance to do things differently. The death may be heart-wrenching or more mundane. Someone who has given up smoking, for example, might dream of burying some cigarettes.

In *Beyond the Pleasure Principle* (1920), Freud wrote that funerals in dreams show a desire for the opposite. A funeral was, therefore, evidence that the dreamer's instinct for life was energized. However, if the funeral is the dreamer's own, Freud said it suggested masochistic tendencies or guilt about something the dreamer had felt was wrong but enjoyed. As you would expect from Freud, this misdeed was very likely sexual.

Questions to ask yourself Ask yourself the following after a nightmare about a funeral:
1. Whose funeral was I attending?
2. What is my relationship with this person?
3. Is this person deceased? Do I bear him or her resentment?

If your answer to the last question is yes, write that person a letter to express your feelings.

Symbolizes change, transitions, letting go, endings

Can this nightmare work positively?

If we were able to say good-bye properly to everyone we lose through death or separation, much of our mental distress would be eliminated. Funerals in dreams allow us to go through the rite of loss in the absence of the person—or object—that has gone. The dream may be upsetting, but its emotion should be embraced and not shunned. Attending a funeral is one of the healthiest nightmares a person can have.

Parapsychological Possibilities in Nightmares

Parapsychological nightmares are dreams that arouse negative emotions, such as fear, bewilderment, and sadness, but that also contain instances of extrasensory perception (ESP). ESP may be reported by a dreamer as a prediction of the future, as telepathy, or necromancy, when the dreamer speaks with someone who has died. Parapsychological nightmares can be very disturbing and frightening, especially so if the events of the nightmare happen in real life, as the dreamer feels that he or she should have done something to prevent the situation from happening.

How dream analysts interpret it There is less evidence for parapsychological nightmares than for parapsychological dreams (see page 78 of Dreams). Researchers have concentrated on nightmares that predict the future, especially ones about catastrophic events and assassination attempts. We do not know why they happen. People who experience them claim to know beyond doubt that they have been forewarned. A warning like this can make the dreamer anxious, but it is best seen as a call to help and support those affected, rather than a chance to stop the event from happening. In a 2002 Internet survey by Paul Blosser, reported by Dr. Laurel Clark, more than half of the participants claimed to have had a precognitive dream. Over 40 percent said they had had numerous precognitive dreams. Twins often report waking from a nightmare with the knowledge that something has happened to their twin. Precognitive, and also telepathic, nightmares can lead to feelings of déjà vu in waking life, when something happens that the dreamer feels sure has already taken place in a dream.

Try this to gain insight If you have a precognitive nightmare, it will be vivid, short, and contain precise detail. People say these dreams feel different and have more impact than others. You can track the concurrence rate between your nightmares and real-life events in your journal. Write a paragraph beside each nightmare, listing areas of your life that might be related. As time passes, you will be able to check events against your prerecorded evidence. You might, for example, dream of someone you haven't seen for years and then, a few days later, bump into them.

Symbolizes undeveloped abilities, omens, paranormal insight

Are there famous examples of precognitive nightmares?

- Abraham Lincoln is said to have had a nightmare in which he was at a funeral. In the nightmare he asked who had died and was told it was the President.

- There were reports of 19 precognitive nightmares from passengers before they boarded the *Titanic*. Some of these people canceled their reservations.

Physical Illness
& Nightmares

We experience some of our worst nightmares when we are physically ill. Illness influences both the content of nightmares and their frequency. These nightmares should not be confused with prodromal nightmares (dreams that foretell physiological illness, see page 79 of Dreams). They take place as a direct result of the dreamer having a fever, being in chronic pain, or being diagnosed with a serious, possibly life-threatening illness.

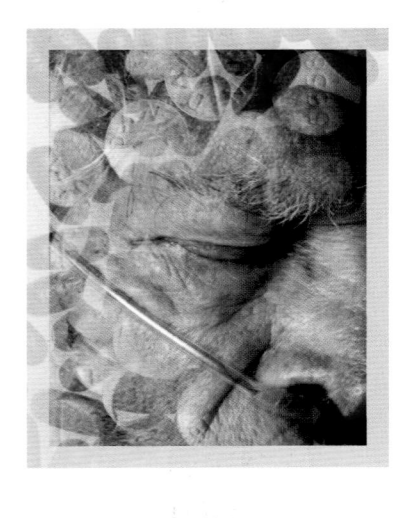

How dream analysts interpret it If you experience an increase in nightmares when you are ill, it can help to establish their cause. You may find it is physiological rather than psychological. A high temperature or fever will induce vivid nightmares from which the dreamer wakes in fear. These nightmares are a result of the fever. They may have no interpretable meaning or may reflect waking worries, such as missing work or being unable to do something you've planned.

Another reason for increased nightmares is experiencing something shocking, such as finding out you have a serious illness. You may need to process what has happened, along with your fear and anxiety. In *Close to the Bone: Life-Threatening Illness as a Soul Journey*, Jean Shinoda Bolen describes how people who have been diagnosed with serious illness experience nightmares as they adapt to the reality that their life may be ending.

Nightmares that follow an extreme medical event, such as an amputation, can reflect the dreamer's denial around the physical change. The dreamer may appear as he or she did before the emergency, then realize that something is wrong and wake up at the point of discovering what this is. These nightmares are part of the important process of adaptation.

Try this to help yourself If you are sick and finding sleep difficult because of nightmares:
1. Recognize that this is your mind's way of adapting to a physical change.
2. Relax and don't fight your body's natural reaction.
3. Most of all, be gentle with yourself. Treat yourself as you would a small child and allow yourself to be sick.

Symbolizes natural physical reaction to illness, adaptation to change

Is my nightmare a reaction to drugs?

Anyone experiencing an increase in unpleasant dreams should establish whether this is due to medication. Although the dreams may be genuinely distressing, it can bring peace of mind to know that the cause is physiological rather than psychological. The drugs used to help with nicotine addiction, for example, are known to lead to an overall increase in dream activity. During the initial phase of nicotine replacement therapy, people frequently report experiencing vivid and disturbing nightmares.

Problem Solving
& Creativity

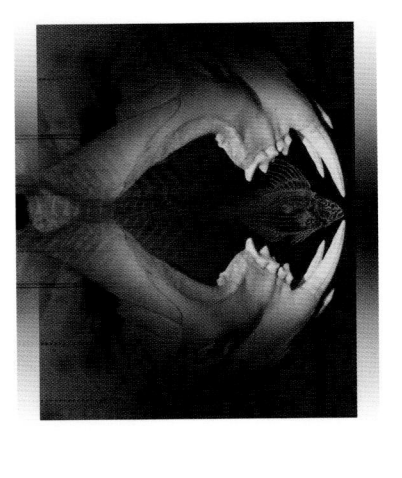

Sometimes you wake from a nightmare with the solution to a seemingly impenetrable problem in front of you. On other occasions, your nightmare needs analysis before you can benefit from its message. The questions suggested on this page are designed to help you do this. If you incubate a dream to find an answer to a problem and you have a nightmare instead, listen to its alarm call. The intensity of the emotion you experienced while asleep suggests you need to take urgent action.

How dream analysts interpret it To gain from a nightmare experience, you need to accept that it has something to offer, then you can look for it. Does an image, symbol, or character stand out? If so, separate it from the emotion of the nightmare and try to establish its meaning. This half of the book shows you how nightmares can be used as a tool to promote well-being.

Julia Cameron, author of *The Artist's Way*, believes we can use creativity to awaken our spiritual lives. She advocates writing three pages of thoughts that come into your head on waking. Adapt this idea by focusing on the dreams or nightmares you had the previous night. Don't try to order or interpret your dreams, just write down what you recall. Your dreaming mind is much freer than your conscious one, and you will be surprised by the ideas you turn out. Writing is an effective way to empty your mind of clutter. If you would prefer not to dwell on your nightmares, you can write them down and leave them behind.

Questions to ask yourself Ask the following questions to uncover the answer the nightmare is trying to give you.

1. How did I react to any threats? Did I face the threat, avoid it, run away? Does this link with my waking life?
2. Were there any, even minor, successes in this dream? (see page 86 of Dreams).
3. If there were any failures, what do they remind me of in waking life? How could I turn around these failures?
4. In an ideal world how could I solve the problem? Rescript the nightmare so it has a positive ending. Tell your new story to someone else. Act on any solutions you identify.

Symbolizes urgency to resolve the waking issue, identification of a problem

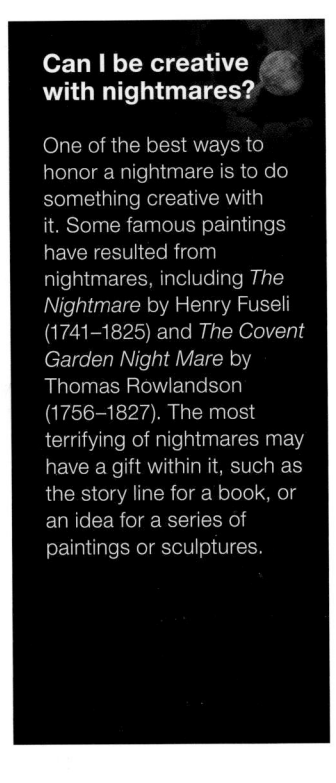

Can I be creative with nightmares?

One of the best ways to honor a nightmare is to do something creative with it. Some famous paintings have resulted from nightmares, including *The Nightmare* by Henry Fuseli (1741–1825) and *The Covent Garden Night Mare* by Thomas Rowlandson (1756–1827). The most terrifying of nightmares may have a gift within it, such as the story line for a book, or an idea for a series of paintings or sculptures.

Unpleasant Dreams

Most of our dreams, not just nightmares, are unpleasant in some way. Researchers have concluded that some uneasiness in a dream is usual. The unpleasant emotions also make a dream more memorable. The jarred notes and anxious moments of normal dreams make them harder to shake off when we get up.

How dream analysts interpret it Bill Domhoff, research professor at the University of California, has identified the elements of an unpleasant dream that indicate psychopathology, or acute mental distress in the dreamer. These deeply unpleasant dreams contain almost no references to friends and almost no friendly interactions with other dream characters. A high level of aggressive interaction adds to the dreamer's distress, especially when the dreamer is the victim. The dreams include a great deal of negative emotion, as well as many misfortunes.

Depressed peoples' dreams are characterized by themes of helplessness, hopelessness, reproach, rejection, and motifs of death. When depression is at its worst, dreams are typically bland and mundane, reflecting the depressed person's view of waking life. Dr. Gerald W. Vogel conducted a study of dreams and depression in 1983 and found that people who have depression also have more REM sleep. Vogel, therefore, deprived a group of depressed people of their REM sleep and found that their waking symptoms improved.

Try this to gain insight Try the following if you have a dream that is unpleasant, but not quite a nightmare:

1. Interpret the symbolism of the dream using the suggestions in the book. Identify the dream's personal meaning.
2. Ask what would happen if this situation reached nightmare proportions in real life? What's the worst that could happen?
3. What would need to take place to make this situation pleasant? What would you ideally like to happen?
4. Ask if you are sitting on the fence in your waking life. Are you not quite miserable but not quite contented either?

Symbolizes current issues, possible depressive content, and the natural order of dream life

When should you let bad dreams be?

If the content of an unpleasant dream doesn't strike you as significant or if it doesn't give you cause for concern, the best course may be to ignore it. The majority of our dreams are unpleasant. Attempts to alter this natural balance may interfere with their function, which we do not as yet fully understand. While it is obviously beneficial to reduce debilitating nightmares, tampering with our dream lives as a whole is not necessary and may be harmful.

Emotions

Research has shown that most of the emotions reported in unpleasant dreams fall into four categories: fear, anger, sadness, or confusion. However, this assumes that there is a recognizable category of dreams that can be labeled unpleasant. In a 2008 study conducted by the Dream Research Group in the U.K., people were asked to sort their dreams into types based on the feelings they experienced while having them. The conclusion was that there is no such thing as an ordinary unpleasant dream (or a pleasant one). As the results below suggest, our dreams are too wide-ranging to be defined this simply.

How dream analysts interpret it The nightmares in the 2008 study were collected from adults between 18 and 25 years old who had just started college. The researchers grouped them as follows:

1. Traditional nightmares associated with threats to survival, such as being chased by a stranger, animal, or a dark figure. The students who reported this dream had recently left home and were learning to live alone for the first time.
2. Nightmares of love and loss. The students who reported such nightmares may have felt that they had lost their parents or other loved ones at home. Their nightmares may have expressed the psychological death of these relationships.
3. Physically bizarre nightmares may, for example, involve pulling wax from a belly button or urinating on kittens—all activities associated with unpleasant feelings. The students who had these nightmares were having new experiences every day. The nightmares reflected their confusion.
4. Bizarre, singular nightmares are the ones that you wake from wondering what the dream was about. The emotion is the main indicator of meaning. The students who reported these dreams were expressing anxiety about their change in circumstances.

Try this to gain insight Rather than reflecting on the individual components of a nightmare, it is sometimes useful to consider the bigger picture. Identify the overall emotional theme and see where in your current life this applies most closely.

Symbolizes current emotional concerns, unacknowledged fears or sadness, anxiety

How do emotions differ in men's and women's nightmares?

A comparison of men's and women's nightmares conducted in 2007 revealed, surprisingly, that men report more threats to their self-esteem (32 percent) than women (8 percent), and also more threats to their integrity (32 percent compared to 16 percent). Women report more threats to survival, however, which might suggest that they fear losing their current identity or sense of self in waking life.

Rejection

People who are experiencing difficulties in waking relationships, particularly intimate ones, often have rejection dreams. It is also a common dream theme for people who experienced childhoods during which they felt unloved. These nightmares force us to relive the feelings of not being wanted. A common example involves the dreamer seeking help from a trusted character and this request being refused. Rejection in a nightmare by someone we trust, particularly someone we love, indicates insecurity in our waking relationship with that person. The most upsetting rejection dreams are often about the dreamer's current partner. In women's nightmares the rejection will frequently have a sexual context or involve the partner having sex with someone else.

How dream analysts interpret it Having nightmares of rejection does not necessarily mean you are being rejected, only that you feel you are or are about to be. The nightmare expresses insecurity. The cause of the dream is usually a past hurt or a betrayal in a previous relationship. In this case the dreamer will have unresolved issues that are beginning to affect a current relationship. Although there is no logic behind believing that a current lover will cheat because a previous one did, the person having the rejection nightmare is showing an inability to trust. These issues need to be addressed in waking life, and may best be dealt with through counseling.

Questions to ask yourself When interpreting your nightmares, there comes a point when it is appropriate to ask what it is you are most afraid of. If your answer is rejection, you can use this nightmare to address your fears. Once attention is paid to rejection dreams, they usually stop. Ask yourself:
1. Where in my life have I felt as if this has happened?
2. Am I afraid that it will happen again?
3. How has this rejection affected my current relationships?
4. Am I looking to any one person for too much security, love, support, reassurance?
5. How can I build healthier support systems? How can I develop friendships with people who care for and value me?

Symbolizes fear of being alone, attachment issues, insecurity

What are the most common dreams about rejection?

The majority of nightmares about rejection concern the dreamer's lover or members of the family. Emotion is at its most raw in dreams featuring current partners, in which the dreamer usually finds out about or sees the partner cheat sexually. Rejection dreams about family members are more subtle. They may involve the family member ignoring a plea for help or refusing to help the dreamer some other way.

Sexual Violence

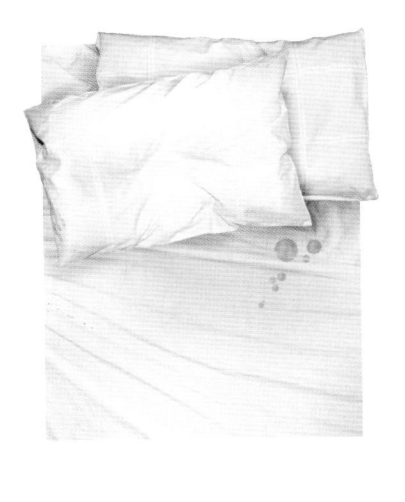

People who have been abused and have a conscious memory of it may have nightmares reflecting their harrowing experiences. These nightmares would fall into the category of post-traumatic nightmares and require treatment by a specialist. In the absence of abuse in real life, dreams of being molested or raped are relatively rare. A frequent question asked of dream therapists is whether a dream of sexual violence could be a hidden memory of an event buried in the dreamer's past. However, if the dreamer cannot recall ever having been abused, no therapist should ever suggest an abuse has taken place solely on the basis of a dream.

How dream analysts interpret it When not referring to real-life events, dreams of this kind can be both shocking and sexually arousing. Dr. Gayle Delaney, who sees clients at the Delaney & Flowers Dream Consultation Center in San Francisco, has identified two kinds of sexual violence in dreams. The first, domination, is reported as a common sexual dream by both men and women. In dreams of domination, the dreamer is playing out pleasurable sexual fantasies while asleep. The other kind of sexual violence belongs firmly in the realm of nightmares. In Delaney's experience these nightmares are experienced only by women, although this may be because men who have suffered abuse have not shared their dream experiences. These dreams are not so much about sex as aggression. They can suggest that the dreamer feels sexually used by someone in waking life. They may also indicate that the dreamer is conditioned to behave submissively, making her easily exploited.

Questions to ask yourself Sexual violence is not really about sex but about the theft of power. If you have this nightmare, ask yourself:
1. Where in my life do I feel violated?
2. What situation in my waking life relates to the feelings in my nightmare?
3. How can I reclaim my power in this situation?

Symbolizes violation, possible abuse issues, victimhood

Only a nightmare?

Nightmares of sexual violence allow us to feel intense feelings of vulnerability, fear, or humiliation, while remaining safe. Ernest Hartmann (see pages 18–19). has written about a series of dreams reported by a woman who was raped. The dreams contain clear central images, including gangs of men, a train coming straight toward her, being caught in a curtain, and a whirlwind. Every image represents terror. Only in her nightmares did the woman feel able to express her emotion around her rape experience.

Aggression

It is impossible to explore aggression in nightmares without referring to Calvin Hall and Robert Van de Castle's work in 1966 on aggressive interactions in dreams. Hall and Van de Castle developed an eight-point system for categorizing incidents of aggression, covering everything from an aggressive thought about another dream character to murder. In nightmares, aggression is most frequently expressed physically. The dreamer might, for example, be assaulted, stabbed, or shot. It is common for aggression to take the form of verbal threats or a chase, in which the terrified dreamer attempts to reach safety while being pursued by another dream character.

How dream analysts interpret it Aggression is an intrinsic feature of most unpleasant dreams and nightmares. It is the most common of all social interactions in dreams, but the darker your dream experience, the more aggression it will contain. It's the aggression in the dream that makes the experience so mentally exhausting. Inevitably, the dreamer is nearly always the victim. Appeals for help are normally refused, leaving the dreamer alone with any number of characters with aggressive intent. In his book *The Multiplicity of Dreams,* Harry Hunt identifies a particularly disturbing aggressive dream that he calls titanic. Titanic dreams, which Hunt suggests are a manifestation of aggression in its most primitive form, typically feature mutilation, dismemberment, and grotesque physical attacks. All these acts are carried out by quasihuman animals, strangers, or the shadow. Fortunately, these types of nightmares are rare.

Questions to ask yourself Understanding the nature of the aggression in a nightmare is one of the most useful things you can do. Once you have identified who initiates the aggression and who is the victim, you are likely to recognize responses that relate directly to your waking life. Ask yourself following:
1. Who is the other person in this aggressive interaction?
2. Who is initiating the aggressive behavior?
3. Do I feel intimidated by this person in waking life?
4. Is this person angry with me, or is it actually me that is angry with this person?

Symbolizes different forms of aggression, repressed anger

How common is aggression in nightmares?

In a study of men's and women's nightmares, conducted in the U.K. in 2008, both men and women reported more incidents of aggression than in their ordinary dreams. In normal dreams, as described by Hall and Van de Castle, aggression occurs in 47 percent of male dreams and 27 percent of female dreams. In nightmares, the statistics rise to 58 percent and 55 percent respectively.

Failure

A failure in a dream may be obvious or be so subtle that you miss it. You might, for example, spend a dream running from one train station to another, then finally reach the airport only to find that you have missed the plane by minutes. Or you might dream of your brother trying to fix his car but not succeeding. Failures are a characteristic of nightmares, along with unpleasant emotions, themes of death, loss, and strangeness.

How dream analysts interpret it For a failure to occur, the dreamer must have a goal. This might be anything from trying to contact a friend to trying to save the world. The important factor is that the dreamer tries to do something and cannot. There is usually a consequence, which can be a pivotal moment. This point may also be when a dream turns into a nightmare.

Dreams of failure reflect an individual's perception of what failure means and the dreamer's gender. This dream was reported by a 23-year-old man and contains traditionally masculine images. *"It went dark, and I could hear gunfire and bombs exploding. I was trying to run away. The buildings were very high and all looked the same and it felt like I was trapped in a tunnel. I could see myself doing these things to try and get out, but nothing worked. I felt so scared, but nothing I did worked. My captors were acting as though I did not exist."* After discussion with a dream therapist, the young man was able to identify where he was at war with the world in his waking life. As the dream illustrates, the situation was both frightening and overwhelming.

Try this to gain insight Attempts to overcome failure often lead to increased anxiety. Examine your nightmares to discover what you are afraid of failing at and compare this with your fears of failure in everyday life. If the failure is accompanied by misfortune, the trickster (see page 43 of Nightmares), or the part of you that sabotages your success, may be doing his work. Ask yourself what you need to do to succeed and whether you are prepared to do it. An example of this dream would be a door that won't open for no apparent reason. The door may open onto success, and you may be inventing reasons for not opening it.

Symbolizes anxiety, fear of failure, attempts to achieve a goal that may be linked to a waking life situation

Can I fail to change my nightmares?

You may experience another kind of failure when attempting to dream lucidly (see pages 32–33 of Dreams). That is, you might fail to achieve full lucidity and to remain asleep. People who are learning to control their dreams are often so shocked by what they are doing that they suddenly wake up. This may happen several times, but do not be discouraged. Lucidity is achievable and, in time, you will be able to relax and enjoy it. Failure of this kind is a natural part of the learning process.

Bad Fortune

Bad fortune, or rotten luck, is what you might expect from a nightmare. Bad things just happen, either to the dreamer or another dream character, and no one will have done anything in the nightmare to cause the problem. As it does in waking life, bad fortune ranges in severity. It can mean trying to fit a key in the lock and the key breaking, the ground suddenly opening up under your feet, or a life-threatening heart attack.

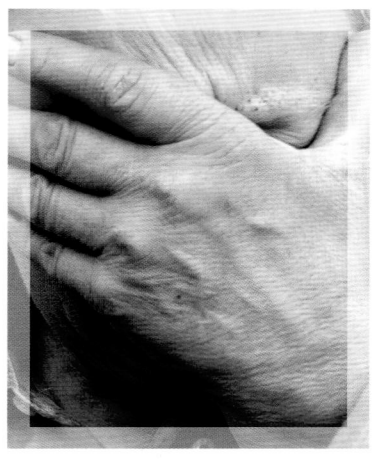

How dream analysts interpret it Researchers have identified various different kinds of misfortune that can occur as part of a dream or nightmare. These may include:

1. Someone, including the dreamer, dying.
2. Someone, including the dreamer, having an illness or injury.
3. Something breaking or getting damaged.
4. An environmental threat, such as a tidal wave.
5. A dreamer or another character feeling as though they are falling or are in danger of falling.
6. A barrier, such as a broken telephone or a locked door.

The most common misfortunes in nightmares are death, serious illness, and accidents. In traditional nightmares the threat to life is based on the actions of another dream character, but bad fortune happens by accident. Antii Revonsou, Professor of Cognitive Science at the University of Skövde in Sweden, thinks these dreams help us rehearse for real life. We use imaginary incidents to prepare or protect ourselves for the worst that can happen. You might dream of someone you love becoming ill, of having a serious accident, or of losing something precious.

Questions to ask yourself No studies have compared people's waking attitudes in terms of how lucky or unlucky they feel in relation to the number of nightmares they have. Misfortune is a chance factor in dreams. However, working with this category of nightmare can reduce bad fortune in future dreams. Start by asking yourself:

1. Do I see the glass as half full or half empty?
2. Do I consider myself to be lucky?
3. Am I delighted by the unexpected, or do I prefer having everything under control?

Symbolizes negative projected thinking, blocks to success

What are the most common examples?

Even normal dreams contain misfortune, and the incidents increase according to the unpleasantness of the dream. The most common type of bad fortune in a nightmare is death or injury, closely followed by obstacles being put in the dreamer's way. In incidents of sleep paralysis (see page 24 of Nightmares), which may be viewed as a type of nightmare, two-thirds of people meet an insurmountable obstacle, typically an inability to speak or move.

"When I say, 'My bed will comfort me, my couch will ease my complaint,' then thou dost scare me with dreams and terrify me with visions, so that I will choose strangling and death, rather than my bones."

Job 7.13–15